How to access the supplemental web r

We are pleased to provide access to a web resource that supple
Fundamentals for Dance. This resource offers vocabulary lists, ext......u icarning activities,
worksheets and answer keys, streaming music clips, and more.

Accessing the web resource is easy!
Follow these steps if you purchased a new book:

1. Visit **www.HumanKinetics.com/MusicFundamentalsForDance**.

2. Click the <u>first edition</u> link next to the book cover.

3. Click the Sign In link on the left or top of the page. If you do not have an
    account with Human Kinetics, you will be prompted to create one.

4. If the online product you purchased does not appear in the Ancillary Items box
    on the left of the page, click the Enter Key Code option in that box. Enter the
    key code that is printed at the right, including all hyphens. Click
    the Submit button to unlock your online product.

5. After you have entered your key code the first time, you will never have to
    enter it again to access this product. Once unlocked, a link to your product will
    permanently appear in the menu on the left. For future visits, all you need to
    do is sign in to the textbook's website and follow the link that appears in the
    left menu!

→   Click the Need Help? button on the textbook's website if you need assistance along
    the way.

How to access the web resource if you purchased a used book:

You may purchase access to the web resource by visiting the text's website,
www.HumanKinetics.com/MusicFundamentalsForDance, or by calling the following:

800-747-4457 . . . . U.S. customers
800-465-7301 . . . . Canadian customers
+44 (0) 113 255 5665 . . . . European customers
08 8372 0999 . . . . Australian customers
0800 222 062 . . . . New Zealand customers
217-351-5076 . . . . International customers

For technical support, send an e-mail to:
support@hkusa.com . . . . U.S. and international customers
info@hkcanada.com . . . . Canadian customers
academic@hkeurope.com . . . . European customers
keycodesupport@hkaustralia.com . . . . .Australian and New Zealand customers

HUMAN KINETICS
The Information Leader in Physical Activity & Health

12-2011

This unique code allows you access to the web resource.

Access is provided if you have purchased a new book.
Once submitted, the code may not be entered for any
other user.

Product: Music Fundamentals for Dance web resource

Key code: HOLLAND-9QTB4P-OSG

Music Fundamentals for Dance

Library of Congress Cataloging-in-Publication Data

Holland, Nola Nolen, 1951-
  Music fundamentals for dance / Nola Nolen Holland.
    p. cm.
  Includes bibliographical references and index.
  ISBN 978-0-7360-9652-2 (soft cover) -- ISBN 0-7360-9652-3 (soft cover)1.Music theory--
Elementary works. 2.Dance music--Analysis, appreciation.I. Title.
  MT7.H7516 2012
  781.02'47928--dc23

                              2012005894

ISBN-10: 0-7360-9652-3 (print)
ISBN-13: 978-0-7360-9652-2 (print)

The web addresses cited in this text were current as of September 2012, unless otherwise noted.

Acquisitions Editor: Gayle Kassing, PhD; **Developmental Editor:** Ragen E. Sanner; **Assistant
Editor:** Anne Rumery; **Copyeditor:** Jan Feeney; **Indexer:** Katy Balcer; **Permissions Manager:** Dalene
Reeder; **Graphic Designer:** Nancy Rasmus; **Graphic Artist:** Tara Welsch; **Cover Designer:** Keith
Blomberg; **Photographer (cover and interior):** Photos courtesy of Dave Garson, unless otherwise
noted; **Art Manager:** Kelly Hendren; **Associate Art Manager:** Alan L. Wilborn; **Illustrations:** ©
Human Kinetics; **Printer:** United Graphics

Printed in the United States of America   10 9 8 7 6 5 4 3 2 1

The paper in this book is certified under a sustainable forestry program.

Human Kinetics
Website: www.HumanKinetics.com

United States: Human Kinetics
P.O. Box 5076
Champaign, IL 61825-5076
800-747-4457
e-mail: humank@hkusa.com

Canada: Human Kinetics
475 Devonshire Road Unit 100
Windsor, ON N8Y 2L5
800-465-7301 (in Canada only)
e-mail: info@hkcanada.com

Europe: Human Kinetics
107 Bradford Road
Stanningley
Leeds LS28 6AT, United Kingdom
+44 (0) 113 255 5665
e-mail: hk@hkeurope.com

Australia: Human Kinetics
57A Price Avenue
Lower Mitcham, South Australia 5062
08 8372 0999
e-mail: info@hkaustralia.com

New Zealand: Human Kinetics
P.O. Box 80
Torrens Park, South Australia 5062
0800 222 062
e-mail: info@hknewzealand.com

E5219

Music Fundamentals for Dance

Nola Nolen Holland

Human Kinetics

Contents

Preface

Since prehistory, whether dancing to their own vocalizations, simple drumming, or a single instrument's accompaniment, people have linked movement to some form of music. To be successful in dancing to music, creating movement for a piece of music, or using music for dance classes, dancers, choreographers, and teachers need to understand the fundamentals of music.

Many years ago I was among a group of dancers learning a choreographer's version of *The Rite of Spring*. Stravinsky's complex music was not explained to us. As we were learning the movement, we also had to memorize the music. Had the répétiteurs been able to analyze the music and break it down into sections, phrases, or counts (even if they were "dancer counts"), our task of learning the movements and their timing with the music would have been so much easier. Left to our own devices, we found that making an entrance at the correct moment in the music became a nerve-racking group activity. Each time we performed, we listened intently. The group's success depended on what seemed to be a nebulous understanding of the music.

More recently, I observed dance history students attempting to re-create a baroque-era step pattern from the dance notation, which was shown below the dance's music. As they counted, they didn't realize that they were actually counting in fives. The dance was supposed to be performed to a 3/4 meter. Their attempt to re-create the step sequence would have been aided by an understanding of music notation.

Because little training in music is offered in dance classes, dancers would benefit from a text that explains the basics of music notation as well as the elements of musical time, melody, texture, reading of scores, and form. *Music Fundamentals for Dance* is such a resource. If you have more than a basic understanding of music, this text provides information and exercises that will further your proficiency. Additionally, the text serves as a reference for choreographers, dance educators, and dancers who seek to become more informed about the relationships between music and dance.

There are many books about dance music or music appreciation; however, after teaching the subject of music for dance, I realized that many basic and requisite topics were missing from available texts. Furthermore, the texts that were *intended* for dance students proved to be too advanced for most dance students. *Music Fundamentals for Dance* is a synthesis of music and dance concepts that is significant in its focus on student dancers, choreographers, and teachers. It will complement classroom instruction and will provide a foundation for further study.

Organization

Music Fundamentals for Dance begins with an introductory chapter on music notation. Chapter 2 presents the fundamentals of musical time, including meter, stress, and accent. The most important thing for both dancers and musicians to know is how the other counts music so that they can collaborate effectively. Chapter 3 explores melody in music and its application to dance composition. Chapter 4 discusses musical texture, contrapuntal devices, and nonimitative polyphony and how the similar concepts of texture in dance add depth and richness to a composition. Chapter 5 discusses the elements of a music score, introduces a variety of music scores and a brief history of each, and examines the usefulness of a music score to dancers, choreographers, and teachers. Chapter 6 presents musical form and structure, such as the introduction, melody, sections of a work, and ending, and how each relates to the sections in a dance composition. Included in this chapter are many classical elements that composers and choreographers continue to use today.

If you are studying to become a dance educator, understanding and mastering the fundamentals of music are essential for two reasons. First, you will need to know about selecting the appropriate prerecorded music for exercises in classes. Second, you will need to know how to communicate with a musician about the kind of music you require for exercises in your classes, such as the meter and quality of the music. Developing the ability to provide varied music will enable you to challenge and inspire your students. Educators and dancers alike have experienced moments when the music elevates an exercise to performance level through the synchronicity of the music and the movement. In this way, this text provides the starting point for future dance educators.

Unique Features of This Book
and Web Resource

Each chapter provides opportunities for further study and for expanding and adapting the topics and subtopics to each user's level of expertise. At the end of each chapter are practical applications suggesting individual and class exercises, class activities, and group or individual projects. Each chapter's web resource materials include a chapter summary, glossary terms and definitions, URLs, extended learning activities for individuals and groups, and forms or worksheets that will help to develop your understanding of music theory.

Instructors' choice of exercises and practical experiences will, of course, depend on their expertise and areas of interest as well as on students' levels of understanding and accomplishment.

On the web resource, chapters have the unique feature of actual music and samples of lyrics, which provide opportunities for class discussion as well as practice in the theories presented in a unit. You will know when a sample of music is available on the web resource when you see the following symbol in the margin (see figure 1).

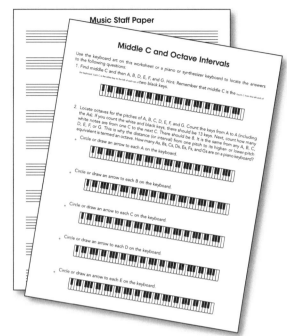

Worksheets and answer keys can be found on the web resource.

Figure 1 Music logo that alerts you to music samples available on the web resource.

Summary

Let's get started on developing your understanding of music. Just like dance, music has a language all its own. Both are nonverbal forms of communication. Just as becoming an excellent dancer, choreographer, or teacher takes time, learning the fundamentals of music takes time. But the rewards of your effort will manifest in your dancing, your choreography, and your teaching. Make an effort not only to read and understand each chapter's material but also to apply what you have read by completing the end-of-chapter exercises, listening to suggested music examples, and using the chapters' web resources. How much you understand music and learn about music will be commensurate with your effort and study.

Acknowledgments

This text was made possible in part by grants from the American Association of University Women Educational Foundation and by two grants from the Pennsylvania State System of Higher Education Faculty Professional Development Council with 100 percent matching funds from Slippery Rock University of Pennsylvania. I am grateful for the fulfillment of my grant requests for this project.

Special thanks go to Mary Margaret Holt, director of the University of Oklahoma School of Dance, for her enthusiasm for my choice of topic for this text. Thanks also to Dr. Allan Ross, University of Oklahoma School of Music. Dr. Ross' advice and suggestions for the text were invaluable.

Without the enduring support and assistance of my parents, this text would have been impossible to achieve. Posthumously to my father, Thomas E. Nolen, and to my mother, Virginia "Ginny" Nolen, words cannot express how much I appreciate all you have done for me. I also wish to thank my daughters, Kiki, Grace, and Hope, for their unconditional love and understanding. Your tolerance, resilience, and adaptability are wondrous.

I must acknowledge the contributions of my husband, Ken Holland, who continually encouraged me to complete the text. His warmth, humor, and belief in me contributed to my strength and resolve in completing the book.

A huge thank-you to the SRU dance students and graduates who gave me permission to use their photos for text illustrations: Zach Bergfelt, Tori Birner, Chelle Blankenship, Melanie Calhoun, Todd Englander, Ashley Lowman, Jessica Madden, Taylor Pearson, Heather Perrow, Amanda Peterson, Josh Pugliese, and Krystie Serviss. Thanks to Jaya Mani, SRU dance faculty member, for granting me permission to use your photograph. Dave and Renee Garson, thank you for your beautiful photographs. Rhyme Chang, your photographic artistry is a great contribution to the text. Thank you!

Thanks to the editors and design staff at Human Kinetics: Gayle Kassing, Ragen Sanner, Anne Rumery, Jan Feeney, Nancy Rasmus, and Dawn Sills. Your determination to get the book to publication was truly inspiring. Your insights and guidance were heartfelt and genuine. I value your expertise and so appreciate your unflagging support.

Since I have been working on this text, every friend and family member has asked if I finished the book. I am not sure if any text is ever truly finished. But for 2012, it is done. Thank you, everyone! Andy Hasenpflug, musician for the SRU department of dance, thank you for your patience in adopting the draft texts year after year for your Music for Dance class! Now you will have a hard copy with proper illustrations for the students. Dr. Glenn Utsch, SRU department of music, thank you for sharing your expertise to help me with reviewing the text.

Basic Concepts of Music and Notation

M usic is part of your craft. It is not to be neglected any more than any other part. It is not something you use per force, like a crutch because you have only one leg. It *is* a leg.

Juli Nunlist,
American composer and pianist (b. 1916)

Notation is a combination of terms, symbols, and signs that enables musicians to reproduce music as the composer wrote it and wishes it to be heard. Even though musicians may not play the music in the exact manner the composer intended, musicians can reproduce the sounds, dynamics, and articulations relatively close to the composer's intent. Musicians must study and understand notation before being able to reproduce the sounds it represents.

In this way, music notation is similar to dance notation. A dance notator (movement analyst or choreologist) must study dance notation in order to reconstruct a dance work as closely as possible to the way the choreographer originally created it. Similar to dance notation, reading music requires study and practice in order to become proficient. Figure 1.1 contains excerpts of music notation and dance notation. Upon studying figure 1.1*b*, note that the Benesh movement notation corresponds to the number of staff lines and bars in the music notation of figure 1.1*a* but obviously not in symbols. In figure 1.1*c*, a Labanotation excerpt, the symbols are entirely different from the music notation. Yet a dance notator would be able to translate the symbols into movement performed with the music. From studying these illustrations, you should be able to see that music notation symbols are as unique as movement notation symbols.

Figure 1.1 *(a)* A piano reduction of the first six measures of Tchaikovsky's Lilac Fairy Variation from the prologue of his score for the Petipa ballet *The Sleeping Beauty*, *(b)* Rhonda Ryman's Benesh movement notation for the same six measures, and *(c)* the Labanotation excerpt.

(a) Reprinted from P. Tchaikovsky, 1890, *La belle au bois dormant* [The sleeping beauty] Op. 66. Piano score (New York: The Tchaikovsky Foundation), 31. *(b)* Reprinted, by permission, of Rhonda Ryman. *(c)* Reprinted, by permission, Dance Notation Bureau and Alfred Publishing Co, Inc.

Lilac Fairy Variation
"The Sleeping Beauty" Prologue

Choreography: Nureyev (1972) after Lopukhov, as taught by Vanessa Harwood (*ca*. 1980)

Music: P. I. Tchaikovsky

b

Six Fairy Variations

Variation 6 - THE LILAC FAIRY
Prologue, Sleeping Beauty

Choreography by M. Petipa, reconstructed by Mary Skeaping
Labanotation by Ann Hutchinson

Enter Before Music | Bars 1 - 15 | Bars 16 - 32 | Bars 32 - 36

c

Figure 1.1 *(continued)*

Staffs

Symbols for musical pitches (or sounds), whether high, medium, or low, appear on a horizontal grouping of five lines and the resulting four spaces between the lines called a **staff** (see figure 1.2). Each line and each space has a letter name that represents a certain pitch as established by the clef (see figures 1.3 and 1.4). Beginning music students learn mnemonic devices to help them remember the names of the lines and spaces in sequence. For the treble staff lines, the mnemonic phrase is "*every good boy does fine.*" The letters assigned to the treble staff spaces spell the word *face*. Similar to the treble staff, the bass staff lines' mnemonic phrase is "*good boys do fine always.*" One of the several mnemonic phrases for the bass staff spaces is "*all cows eat grass.*"

For pitches that are higher or lower than those represented by the staff's five lines and four spaces, one or more **ledger lines** indicate higher and lower pitches (see figure 1.5). Notice the use of ledger lines and consequent spaces in figure 1.5.

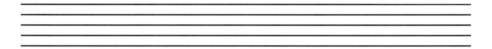

Figure 1.2 A music staff.

Figure 1.3 The treble staff.

Figure 1.4 The bass staff.

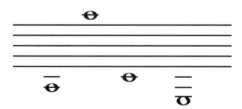

Figure 1.5 Examples of ledger lines.

Pitch

The first seven letters of the alphabet (A through G) name the seven pitches used in Western music notation. They move from lower to higher pitches as A through G repeat in sequence.

The term **pitch** refers to the highness or lowness of tones determined by a musical sound's frequency. Each musical pitch has a specified frequency measured in **Hertz** (named after the 19th-century physicist who established the existence of sound wavelengths, Heinrich Hertz). Each pitch has a specified number of Hertz (Hz) per second. For example, the A to which bands or orchestras tune before the conductor's entrance at a concert vibrates at a rate of 440 Hz. In other words, the speed of the auditory wavelength—the number of vibrations per second (440 vibrations per second in the case of the tuning A)—determines the pitch.

Instrumentalists learn how to produce the pitches represented by music notation on their instruments. Vocalists also learn how to sing the pitches as they relate to notes on the staff. For example, violinists, pianists, and clarinetists know how to produce the pitches indicated by the music through knowing the fingerings, where their fingers are placed on their instruments. Generally, instrumentalists will have consecutive single staffs to read whether they are playing as a soloist or with an ensemble (see figure 1.6).

Just as Western language is read from left to right, Western music is read from left to right and from the top left of a page to the bottom right of a page. Once musicians know how to read the pitches as indicated on printed music and where the pitches are located on an instrument, they can begin to play music.

Figure 1.6 Sample staff of music for one instrument, a baroque-era dance, a bourrée by Johann Kuhnau (1660-1722).

Reprinted from J. Kuhnau, 1689, Bourée. In *Dance movements by old masters*, edited by W. Hillemann (London: Schott & Co. Ltd.).

Three Clefs

A **clef** is a symbol placed at the beginning of a staff. Each clef assigns certain pitches to the lines and spaces of the staff. There are three clefs in music notation with which dancers should be familiar: the **G clef (treble clef)**, the **F clef (bass clef)**, and the **C clef (alto or tenor clef)**. Knowing the clefs helps a dancer read a musical score and discern the pitches the instruments are to play. (For more examples of clef notation, see chapter 5.)

G Clef (or Treble Clef)

The G clef is commonly known as the treble clef. The term *G clef* evolved because the clef was derived from an old-fashioned letter G. In general, the G clef is used in music written for higher-pitched instruments and voices such as violins, woodwinds (flutes, clarinets, oboes, saxophones), the right hand on the piano (the upper half of the piano keyboard from middle C to the right), and women's voices (soprano, mezzo-soprano, alto). The G clef crosses the G line four times, centers on the second line (the G line) of the treble staff, and names that line G (see figure 1.7).

Figure 1.7 The G clef, also known as the treble clef.

One exception to G clef usage is in French violin music. The G clef moves to become centered on the lowest line of the treble staff, the E line. As a result, the **French violin clef**, which is identical in appearance to the G clef, renders the G clef a moveable clef. The G clef, therefore, when positioned for the French violin, becomes known as the French violin clef and indicates that the first line of the staff is the G above middle C.

F Clef (or Bass Clef)

The F clef is also referred to as the bass clef and is named the F clef because the symbol is a derivation of an old-fashioned letter F. The two vertical dots, one above the F line and one below, frame the F line of the bass staff as well (see figure 1.8). The bass clef designates staffs for lower-pitched brass instruments, the cello and double bass in the string family, baritone and bass men's voices, and keyboard music for the left hand. For the baritone and the contrabass or sub-bass clefs, the F clef centers on the D and A lines of the bass staff, respectively. This shift in the F clef's placement on the bass staff as the baritone and contrabass clefs renders the F clef a moveable clef very similar to the way a G clef moves its staff placement for French violin music.

Figure 1.8 The F clef, also known as the bass clef.

C Clef (Alto, Tenor, or Soprano Clef)

The C clef (alto, tenor, or soprano clef) may be less familiar even to dancers who have studied music. It is a moveable clef, which means that the center of the clef, the point, may go on lines of the staff other than the center line. No matter which line the clef's center points to, that line is middle C.

The C clef appears primarily in baroque- and classical-era vocal and instrumental music. In music for the viola, the point of the C clef goes on the third line of the staff (see figure 1.9*a*), while in music for the cello, bassoon, or trombone, it goes on the fourth line (see figure 1.9*b*). The C clef will appear in music for string quartets, quintets, and symphonies as well as in jazz music (depending

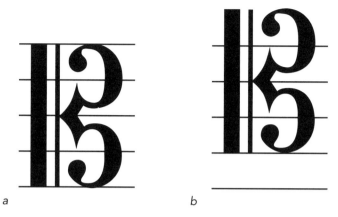

a   *b*

Figure 1.9 *(a)* The C clef, also known as the alto clef, as used in music for the viola; *(b)* the C clef, shown as the tenor clef, which is used in music for the cello, bassoon, and trombone.

on the instrumentation). Dancers need to be familiar with the two things that a C clef indicates: the center of the clef indicates middle C and the instruments whose music employs the C clef. In chapter 5, Reading Music Scores, you will see this clef repeatedly.

Grand Staff

Pianists learn how the clefs assign pitches to the piano keys via the treble and bass staff lines and spaces just as other instrumentalists and vocalists do for their instruments. A **grand staff** is the music notation format for keyboard music (see figure 1.10). Music for piano, organ, harpsichord, clavichord, or electric keyboard employs grand staffs. In choral music and vocals for musical theater, the piano's grand staff is below the singers' staffs and is linked to them by bar lines so that the pianist and vocalists stay together as they are reading through or performing the music.

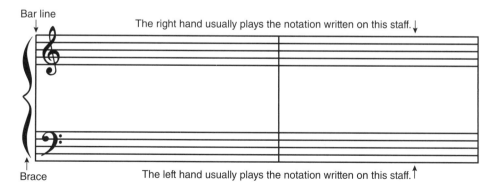

Figure 1.10   The grand staff with brace and bar lines.

For the grand staff, two staffs, one above the other, are linked at the beginning of a composition by a brace and a bar line. Throughout notated keyboard music, bar lines run vertically through both staffs. A heavy double bar line at the end of and through both staffs signals the end of the composition. For the grand staff, the top staff, or treble staff, represents the pitches above middle C, which are usually assigned to the right hand. On the lower staff, or the bass staff, pitches below middle C are notated and are usually played by the left hand. Of course, a composer might want both hands to play pitches above or below middle C. In this case, both the top and bottom staffs will have treble or bass clefs at the beginning of the staffs as in piano duet music where one pianist plays music generally notated above middle C (the primo part) while a second pianist plays music notated below middle C (the secondo part). The primo part has G clefs at the beginning of each staff while the secondo part will have F clefs at the beginning of each staff.

On a page of music, each consecutive grand staff begins with a brace and a bar line. The brace of the grand staff connects the treble and bass staffs. It looks similar to a left curly bracket and indicates that the pianist plays both the treble and bass staffs at the same time. The bar line, when used in a grand staff, is the vertical line that follows the brace. It extends from the top line of the treble staff to the bottom line of the bass staff. It also links the right-hand part and the left-hand part and aids the pianist in reading both staffs simultaneously. The treble staff and bass staff pitches and notes are identified in figure 1.11 with arrowed lines pointing out their corresponding keys on the keyboard. The illustration also points out the brace and first bar line of the grand staff as well as an ending double bar.

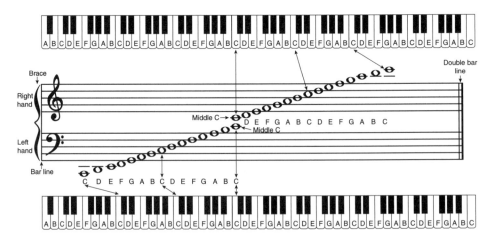

Figure 1.11 A grand staff with pitches shown as they relate to the piano keyboard. See the accompanying web resource to view the figure in its full size.

Middle C

Middle C is at the center of the grand staff. It represents the most central C on the piano keyboard (see figure 1.12) and is the approximate middle of a piano keyboard's 88 keys. On an actual piano, middle C is usually just to the left of the name of the piano's maker.

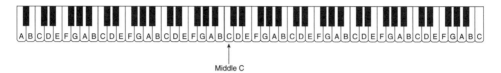

Figure 1.12   Middle C delineated on the piano keyboard and the names of the piano keys' pitches. See the accompanying web resource to view the figure in its full size.

Notes and Rests

In music notation, notes indicate pitch and duration. Rests indicate the length of silence. There are many symbols for notes and rests. The following discussion covers basic notation for notes and rests.

Types of Notes

Notes are musical symbols that serve a dual purpose. First, a note's location on a staff determines the pitch a musician or singer produces, whether it is a high, medium, or low tone. Second, notes have a time value. They determine how long the sound lasts. This second point, time values for notes, is discussed in chapter 2. For now, let's learn the basics about notes.

A **whole note** looks like a small, empty, slightly oval circle. The note is a whole note if the note head (the circular or oval part of the note) has no **stem** (a stem is a short, straight line attached to the right or left side of the note head). If a note looks like a whole note with a downward stem attached to the left side or an upward stem on the right, it is a **half note**. A half note becomes a **quarter note** when the note head is completely black. Similar to the half note, a quarter note may have a right-side upward or a left-side downward stem (see figure 1.13).

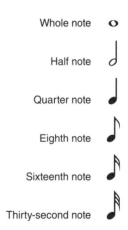

Whole note

Half note

Quarter note

Eighth note

Sixteenth note

Thirty-second note

Figure 1.13   Names and types of notes.

Further divisions of note values progress mathematically as indicated by symbols on a note's stem. These symbols, known as **flags**, are placed at the top of the stem and are always to the right of the stem whether the stem is up or down. One flag added to the stem of a quarter note makes it an **eighth note**. Two flags designate a **sixteenth note**, and so on, up to five flags, indicating a one-hundred-twenty-eighth note. The name of a type of note never changes. Therefore, based on the appearance of the note (whether it is black or not) and its stem characteristics, a musician can determines the note's value within a time signature. (Time signatures are discussed in chapter 2.)

Types of Rests

Rests are musical symbols that denote a period of silence between sounds (pitches). Obviously, rests do not represent pitches because there is no sound for the duration of a rest. In this way, rests are different from notes. Yet, for each note value, there is a corresponding rest, which indicates silence. Rests carry the same names as notes of the corresponding value, although the symbols for rests differ from those for notes. They also have equivalent time values as their counterpart notes. Figure 1.14 shows the most commonly used rests.

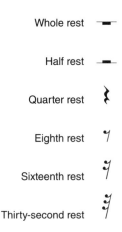

Whole rest

Half rest

Quarter rest

Eighth rest

Sixteenth rest

Thirty-second rest

Figure 1.14 Names and types of rests.

Tonality

Much of the music we are familiar with originated in the common practice period (1600-1900 CE), which includes the baroque, classical, and romantic eras. Also included in these "common practices" is the use of the **major** and **minor** tonal system. Both the major and minor scales (modes) have a specified pattern of whole and half steps (Canada and the United Kingdom use the terminology *tones* and *semi-tones* instead of the terms *whole steps* and *half steps*), which determine the pitches of the scale. A **half step** is from one key to the very next on a keyboard. A **whole step** skips one key. A **scale** is a series of alphabetically arranged pitches, which usually progress by steps and half steps. Therefore, knowing the step patterns of the major and minor scales enables identification of mode. In other words, a scale's step pattern reveals its mode as being major or minor.

An **interval** is the number of pitches between one pitch and another including the two pitches. The respective pitches may sound simultaneously or in sequence, one after the other. An interval refers to how close or far apart two pitches are.

One of the standard intervals that occurs in music is the **octave**. The term *octave* is derived from Latin and means "eight." From the first pitch of a scale to the last is an interval of eight scale-determined steps and half steps as discussed earlier. Every major and minor scale has eight pitches. A chromatic scale includes every half step in an octave for a total of 13 pitches counting the first and last notes of the scale. Whole-tone scales have seven pitches and pentatonic scales have five. A scale begins and ends on its key center pitches. In the key of C, the scale's first and last pitches would be Cs. The first pitch of an ascending scale is an octave lower than the final pitch.

Musicians count the first and last pitch in any interval. Therefore, as one pitch is followed by another or as two pitches sound simultaneously, the distance between the two pitches also names the interval. The earlier example of an octave in the key of C, from one C to the next, allows us to discern other intervals. Moving up the scale from C to D, the second pitch of a C scale, is an interval of a second. From C to the third pitch of the scale, E, is an interval of a third and so on.

Two pitches sounded together form a harmonic interval known as a dyad. Chords have three or more tones. The simultaneous playing of various pitches creates **harmony** between the pitches. Harmony may be consonant or dissonant depending on the intervals of the sounding pitches. **Consonant** intervals sound pleasant and agreeable to most listeners while **dissonant** intervals may seem incongruous or grating. Now let's talk about tonality in general.

Tonality refers to the key center of a piece of music. Music using primarily the pitches of the C scale, for example, is said to be in the key of C. Because of the various tonalities available for use in world music, there are numerous types. For example, the tonality of Western music will differ from Japanese **gagaku** music, which is classical Japanese court music. Jazz music employs chord structures and harmonies based on Western music's system of steps and half steps. These are quite different from the quarter tones and dissonant drones of gagaku. The tonality of non-Western popular music is informed by the music of the culture from which it emerges. Additionally, in the last century, composers created atonal works, which are devoid of a key center as well as the harmonies that come from basing music in a particular key. Before discussing keys, you need to understand the concept of accidentals and how a composer uses them in a composition.

Accidentals: Altering Pitch

When composers want to alter a pitch or several pitches within the tonality of a piece of music, they use symbols termed **accidentals** (see figures 1.15 and 1.16). An accidental produces a half-step change in pitch. By placing a **sharp**, a **flat**, or a **natural** in front of a note, a composer shifts the pitch. A sharp raises a note one half step. A flat lowers a note one half step. A natural cancels a previous sharp or flat. For example, the key signature of C major has no sharps or flats. Therefore, an accidental, when used before one of the pitches in the

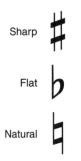

Sharp

Flat

Natural

Figure 1.15 Names and types of accidentals.

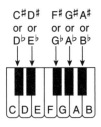

Figure 1.16 Sharps and flats on a piano keyboard.

key of C major, changes the way that particular note sounds. Accidentals can add color, flavor, mystery, or humor to music. Additionally, accidentals produce chromatic alterations. They affect the pitch of the tone in the music. Note the accidentals in the excerpt of staccato music in table 1.4 later in this chapter.

Key Signatures and Keys

Key signatures may be a single sharp or flat or a collection of sharps or flats placed at the beginning of a musical composition to indicate the key. The key of C is the only exception to the use of sharps or flats to indicate a key signature. The key of C has no sharps or flats. So when musicians or singers see no sharps or flats at the beginning of a piece of music, they know the music is in the key of C. When used in key signatures, sharps and flats are no longer termed *accidentals*. The group of sharps or flats represents the basic key of the piece of music. Therefore, music in a certain key has specific sharps or flats, which apply throughout the piece of music with the exception of the use of accidentals or a change of the key within the composition. Note how the tonic pitches, the first note of each scale, for the keys of D and F major are the respective pitches that name the key (see figure 1.17). At the beginning of a piece of music, the *clef*, *key* signature, and *time* signature are in alphabetical order on the music staff: c, k, and t. (Information on time signatures is in chapter 2.)

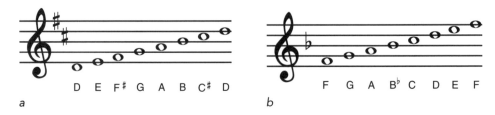

a   b

Figure 1.17 Sample key signatures and scales for (a) D major and (b) F major.

Major and Minor Modes

The major and minor scales are pitch patterns and aural perceptions that are easy or difficult to hear depending on the listener's music skills. The **major scale** sounds happy or cheerful to some, while the **minor scale** sounds melancholy or brooding. Many of Western culture's traditional melodies are rooted in the major and minor modes, which delineate the pitch vocabulary used for those melodies. In Western music, a melody or theme is frequently rooted in one of these two modes. (Refer to the previous section on tonality. Chapter 3 provides a detailed discussion of melodies and themes.)

TRACK 1:
Major scale.

TRACK 2:
Natural minor scale.

TRACK 3:
Harmonic minor scale.

TRACK 4:
Melodic minor scale.

TRACK 5:
Music in a major mode: "My Baby's Foxtrot" by E. Swann.

TRACK 6:
Music in a minor mode: "Melodrama" by R. Webb.

Each scale also has a specified step pattern, as discussed earlier. For example, the major mode's step pattern is two whole steps followed by one half step followed by three whole steps, concluding with one half step. There are three common minor modes (natural, harmonic, and melodic), each with its respective whole- and half-step pattern. Listen to Mozart's "Rondo alla Turca" (also known as "Turkish Rondo" or "Turkish March"). Can you determine the tonality of the first section of the rondo? What about the second section? Do they have the same tonality? What about the third section? There are many examples of easily discernable and difficult-to-hear tonalities in familiar tunes. Listen to the tune "Hearts and Flowers" from the late 19th century. Is it in major or minor mode? What do you think the tonalities are for Duke Ellington's "East St. Louis Toodle-Oo" and George Gershwin's "Summertime" or "It Ain't Necessarily So"?

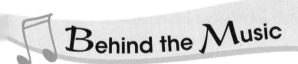

Theodore Moses Tobani's "Hearts and Flowers"

Do you recognize this famous tune? In cartoons, it has been used when a character is crying profuse tears. It was also a standard for pianists and organists accompanying silent movies in the early 20th century. Although "Hearts and Flowers" sounds sad, it is actually written in a major key. The song's second section was often used as a villain's theme in films.

Dynamics

Dynamics refer to the general loudness or softness of a piece of music or a section of music. In other words, dynamics refer to the volume or sound level of the music. Dynamic indications, through terms usually in Italian (see table 1.1) and symbols (see table 1.2), are approximate volume levels and depend on the instrumental or vocal group and the music's style.

These terms and symbols indicating dynamics are important to the dancer, choreographer, or teacher because they affect the listener's perception of the music. Therefore, dynamics may influence how a dancer reacts to music. Dynamics may also influence a choreographer's choice of movement. How a composer has established the dynamic levels of music may also influence how a music educator teaches the music to students or how a dance educator guides students through compositional exercises and structures.

Listen to a recording of a baroque composition played by a period ensemble. Then listen to the same piece of music performed by a modern symphony orchestra. How does your perception of the dynamics from the period ensemble's performance compare to your perception of the dynamics of the modern orchestra's performance? Next, listen to a classical-era piece performed by a period ensemble and then by a modern symphony orchestra. Consider or discuss the variations in dynamics. Are they as obvious? Or are the dynamic differences more subtle or difficult to hear? Does a *piano* or *forte* marking sound the same from one recording to the other? Taking this concept of music dynamics into dance performance, would a sound system's speaker placement and the sound level affect the audience's or performers' perception of the dynamic markings? Possibly? How and why?

Table 1.1 Terms Indicating Dynamics

Notation	Term	Meaning
ppp	pianississimo	very, very soft
pp	pianissimo	very soft
p	piano	soft
mp	mezzo piano	moderately soft
mf	mezzo forte	moderately loud
f	forte	loud
ff	fortissimo	very loud
fff	fortississimo	very, very loud

Table 1.2 Symbols Indicating Dynamics

Symbol	Term	Abbreviation	Meaning
< (crescendo)	crescendo	*cresc.*	gradually becoming louder
> (decrescendo)	decrescendo or diminuendo	*decresc.* or *dim.*	gradually becoming softer
sfz	sforzando	*sfz*	sudden emphasis on a single note or chord

Terms and Symbols of Expression

In music, terms are used to indicate the expressiveness with which music is to be performed. Using an expression term at the beginning of a piece of music indicates a general mood and, in some cases, an expression term might indicate speed (tempo). See table 1.3 for a short list of these terms. Expression terms and symbols may also be inserted anywhere in the music when a composer desires a change of mood, tempo, volume, or quality. (Tempo markings are discussed in chapter 2.) Table 1.3 provides a list of some common terms of expression and symbols along with their meanings.

Table 1.3 Terms for Musical Expression

Term	Meaning
accelerando (accel.)	becoming faster
agitato	agitated
animato	animated
assai	very (used with other terms)
con	with (used with other terms)
con brio	with spirit
dolce	sweetly
grazioso	graceful
maestoso	majestic
poco	little
poco a poco	little by little
scherzando	playful

Articulation

Articulation markings tell a musician or a singer how to begin to play or sing a tone and how to end it. Composers and musicians refer to the beginning of a sound as **attack**. They term the ending of a sound (tone) as **release**. Articulation manifests in the attack and release as well as the type of accent a note receives.

Dynamic Accent Marks

When composers want to give extra emphasis to notes, they use accent marks. Table 1.4 shows the five basic dynamic **accent** marks: *staccato*, *staccatissimo*, *marcato*, *martelato,* and *tenuto*. Note how two or more of the dynamic accents are sometimes present in the same musical excerpts. As shown in the table, **staccato** literally means "detached." **Staccatissimo** means "most staccato." **Marcato** means "marked." **Martelato** means "hammered." **Tenuto** is based on one of the forms of the Italian word *tenere,* meaning "to hold." Each accent mark indicates a very specific treatment of a note. Eight further combinations of the five basic accent marks permit even more precision in executing and accenting a note.

TRACK 8:
Music using staccato: "Bransles" by C.K. Palmer.

Table 1.4 Dynamic Accent Marks

Musical term (Italian)	Meaning	Symbol
staccato	Shortens a note by half of its value, separates it from the following note, and is placed above or below the note	•
staccatissimo	An elongated, triangular accent above or below a note that shortens a note to a quarter of its time value and the remainder of its time value is given to silence	▼

Musical term (Italian)	Meaning	Symbol
marcato	A normal, percussive accent in which a note receives a strong emphasis followed by lowered volume	

| martelato | Similar to marcato, but a percussive and strong accent with more separation between notes; a form of staccato | |

| tenuto | A legato accent that indicates a note should be played to its full value | - |

Staccato reprinted from P. Tchaikovsky, 1878, *Violin concerto in D major*, Op. 35 (New York: Edwin F. Kalmus), 48. Marcato reprinted from W.A. Mozart, 1783, Turkish march. In *Piano pieces the whole world plays*, Vol. 2 (New York: Appleton-Century-Crofts), 38. Martelato reprinted from X. Scharwenka, 1877, Polish dance in E flat minor, Op. 3, No. 1. In *Piano pieces the whole world plays* (New York: Appleton-Century-Crofts), 95. Tenuto reprinted from S. Rachmaninoff, 1893, Prelude in C sharp minor, Op. 3, No. 2. In *Piano pieces the whole world plays*, Vol. 2 (New York: Appleton-Century-Crofts), 101.

Legato

TRACK 9: Music using legato: "Barbara Allen" by G. Dorset.

Legato means "bound." Legato playing is the norm for musicians. They play music, connecting one sound to the next, as a standard performance practice. An additional reminder to play legato is called a **slur**, a curved line placed over or under the notes, which may also indicate **phrasing** (phrasing means that the notes are linked as a musical thought very similar to a sentence in language). When linked by legato symbols, notes sound smoothly connected.

Notice the legato or slur markings in figure 1.18. The treble staff markings in the first measure connect the G-to-E note groupings and the A-to-F groupings in the second measure. On the bass staff, the shorter legato markings connect the C to E in the first measure and the C to D in the second measure (see figure 1.18). Built on Bach's Prelude no. 1 in C major, BWV 846, from *The Well-Tempered Clavier Book I*, the famous Bach-Gounod "Ave Maria" provides a vocal example of legato. An Internet search will bring up many audio clips of Bach's Prelude and the Bach-Gounod Ave Maria. Also listen to Rachmaninoff's Vocalise as an additional example of legato vocal articulation or Barbra Streisand's vocalise-style recording of Gabriel Fauré's Pavane for Orchestra and Chorus ad lib in F-sharp minor, op. 50.

Figure 1.18 Legato markings in the opening two measures of Bach's Prelude no. 1 in C major.

Reprinted from J.S. Bach, 1722, Prelude in C [No.1] from the well-tempered clavier, BWV 846. In *Piano pieces the whole world plays*, Vol. 2 (New York: Appleton-Century-Crofts), 26.

Summary

Music notation is a language all its own. It uses prescribed and unique symbols to convey this language. Even its basic concepts can seem complex. To learn about music in a short time is to study and understand what has evolved through centuries of musical eras. This chapter has highlighted common musical notations and concepts that dancers should know: staffs, clefs, pitch, notes and rests, tonality, and dynamic and articulation markings. This information provides a basic foundation for understanding music notation. Continue your music studies by learning about musical time in chapter 2.

Before you proceed, there are exercises, discussion points, and activities for this chapter's content here and on the web resource. Completing and practicing these will give you a better working knowledge and understanding of concepts presented in chapter 1.

Practical Applications

Supplementary Exercises and Activities

1. Practice clapping in time with a metronome. Do you tend to rush your clapping and get ahead of the metronome's pulse? Clap four pulses at forte. Clap four pulses at piano. Alternate, beginning with four pulses of piano followed by four pulses of forte. Then, beginning with piano, can you clap four pulses that increase in volume to a fifth pulse that is the loudest (crescendo) and decrease the next three clapped pulses in volume (decrescendo)? On a piece of paper, practice drawing the dynamic symbols for crescendo and decrescendo several times each. Also, write the abbreviations for crescendo and decrescendo.

2. Listen to various popular songs, world music, jazz, or classical music. Try to determine whether each piece of music sounds as if it is a major or minor mode or whether it alternates between the two modes throughout the song or piece of music. Select one or two examples to play for the class. Be prepared to support your opinion on why the music is major or minor mode. If you have difficulty hearing the difference between the major and minor modes, listen to Mozart's "Rondo alla Turca" in class and discuss whether it is major or minor. Also listen to Chopin's Prelude in C Minor, op. 28, no. 20, and his "Funeral March" from Sonata no. 2 in B-flat, op. 35, no. 2, both of which are in the minor mode.

3. Bring a favorite piece of music or a favorite song to play for the class. As a class, determine whether the music's mode is major or minor. While you are or the class is listening, tap your finger or your foot. How would you count the music? Does it sound as if it is organized in twos, threes, or fours? This exercise is in preparation for chapter 2 about musical time.

4. Replay some of the music you heard in class or discussed in this chapter. Which dynamic and expression terms might apply to the music? If your class received copies of specific music, highlight or circle the dynamic and expression markings. Reminder: Some of the expression markings may also refer to or affect the music's tempo. Refer to chapter 2 for a discussion of tempo.

For additional assignments, handouts, web links, and more, please visit the web resource at www.HumanKinetics.com/MusicFundamentalsForDance.

Elements of Musical Time

*P*erhaps of all the most basic elements of music, rhythm most directly affects our central nervous system.

George Crumb,
American composer (b. 1929)

Musical time is organized in three ways: through pulse, meter, and rhythm. This chapter defines pulse, beat, and meter and explains rhythm and other elements of musical time. Because dancers often count music by measures or half measures, you need to know that musicians must count every note in the music. It would be virtually impossible to move to every count or subdivision of a count in a fast passage of music. Yet the most important thing for both dancers and musicians to know is how the other counts music so that they can collaborate effectively.

To begin to understand rhythm, you must first understand pulse, beat, and meter. You can then study other areas of time, such as tempo, rhythmic notation, syncopation, and polyrhythm. This chapter also introduces these topics. Before embarking on these discussions, however, you must first understand the difference between pulse and beat.

Pulse

A **pulse** is regularly occurring but is unorganized by accents. Examples of a pulse are a dripping faucet, walking at a steady pace, or a regular heartbeat. Pulse has no meaning until it is organized into accented (or strong) and unaccented (or weak) beats. Human body movements as well as movements from nature often inspire pulse and rhythm.

Metrical Accent

Again, a dripping faucet, even-paced walking, and a heartbeat are examples of an unorganized but regular pulse. If the drips, steps, or heartbeats are organized into units of twos or threes (two drips, two steps, three heartbeats), the musical practice is to place an emphasis on the first of each grouping. Once pulses are organized in groups, they are termed *beats*. Remember that Western music forms tend to place an emphasis on the first beat of each grouping, which is called a **metrical accent**.

Stress

Returning to the examples of dripping water and walking, a **stress** occurs when a beat in a sequence of beats receives an emphasis. A stress is usually applied to a beat other than the first.

Beat

When pulses are counted within a metric context, they are referred to as *beats*. **Beats** divide time into equal durations. Beat is the number of pulses between regularly occurring accents. The organization of pulses, therefore, means applying regularly occurring accents to establish the music's meter, or its beat. Pulses occur evenly. Yet, until the pulses are organized with regularly occurring accents, they remain pulses as in the earlier examples of dripping water, a walk, and a steady heartbeat. Therefore, **meter** is a series of pulses receiving a regularly occurring accent on count 1, which then designates them as beats. A composer, when applying a regularly occurring accent, consciously establishes the music's meter. Therefore, establishing meter also distinguishes pulses as beats. To transition from this discussion of pulse and beat to how beats are organized in measures, you must know what meter is. But first you need to know about the space between bar lines, the measure.

Measure

A measure is the space on the staff between the bar lines. It is composed of notes, rests, accents, and stresses. A measure's length depends on the music composition's time signature. The tempo of the music also determines how long a measure lasts. Therefore, a measure is a metrical unit.

Because of measures' beginning and ending bar lines, measures are also known as *bars*. A classically trained musician is more likely to use the term *measure,* while popular or jazz musicians might refer to measures as *bars.* Both terms are acceptable and interchangeable. As long as the time signature remains the same throughout a piece of music, each measure will have the same number of beats per measure.

Time Signature

The **time signature,** also known as **meter signature,** of a piece of music defines how the beat is organized by prescribing how many beats occur per measure and what kind of note designates one beat. Each beat is counted sequentially. Beginning with the first beat, a musician may count 1, 2, 3, 4, and so on depending on what the top number is in the time signature. The top number in time signatures reflects the number of beats in regular, repeated groupings of beats in each measure (see figure 2.1). By creating consistent groupings of beats, or by using measures with the same number of beats, music has a feeling of an even flow or pace. In music with more complex mixed meters where the time signature may change from measure to measure, the music's flow may feel irregular. In music with an asymmetrical meter such as 5/4, beats can be stressed in a variety of combinations. A discussion of counting asymmetrical meter occurs later in this chapter.

Figure 2.1 Time signatures.

A time signature notation does two things: The top number indicates how many beats occur per measure, and the lower number gives the type of note that will receive one beat (see figure 2.2). For example, if the time signature is 4/4, the upper number indicates that there are four beats per measure. The lower number, in this case the numeral 4, tells the musician that a quarter note receives one beat. Two exceptions to time signatures with two numerals are the symbols for common time (simple quadruple meter, or 4/4) and cut time (*alla breve*, simple duple meter, or 2/2; see figure 2.3). In general, common time, or 4/4 meter, is the most common meter used in music, especially popular music, rock, rap, and hip-hop.

To reiterate, a time signature designates how many beats in a measure and what kind of note receives one beat. Because time signatures have one number written above and below the middle line of the staff, they look similar to fractions at the beginning of a piece of music. Since there is not really a line separating the numbers, 3/4 time is not referred to as "three fourths" time. It is called "three four" time.

As previously stated, the bottom number on the time signature is the number that designates what kind of note receives 1 beat. It can be a variety of note values, as in 2/4 (4 representing a quarter note), 6/8 (8 representing an eighth note), or 2/2 (2 representing a half note). Sometimes, though rarely, composers will use a 16 representing the sixteenth note or a 1 representing the whole note in time signatures. Often, it is a four representing a quarter note.

In the 20th century, composers created additional time signatures, making exceptions to the standard two-numeral time signature. Along with the new

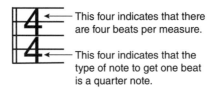

Figure 2.2 Explanation of the 4/4 time signature.

Figure 2.3 Equivalent symbols for *(a)* common time, a symbol that also indicates a 4/4 time signature; and *(b)* cut time (alla breve), an alternative symbol that indicates a 2/2 time signature.

time signatures, composers created new ways of notating them. These new time signatures might have the lower number replaced by a note value. Additionally, composers created decimal meters, fractional meters (i.e., 2½/4 and 5½/4), and polymeters during the 20th century. See the following discussion on various meter classifications for information on mixed meters and polymeters.

Basic Meter Classifications: Simple and Compound

The basic types of meter classifications are simple and compound. Simple or compound meters occur with two (duple), three (triple), or four (quadruple) beats per measure. In **simple meter**, the top number is always 2, 3, or 4, and the beat unit divides into two equal parts. (A beat unit is another way of saying the number of beats in the measure.) For **compound meter**, the top number is always 6, 9, or 12, and the beat unit divides into three equal parts.

Following are some examples of duple, triple, and quadruple simple and compound meters:

- 2/4 meter is a simple duple meter. It is counted 1, 2. It has two beats per measure, and the quarter note receives one beat. In duple meter, the metrical accent is on the first beat, or count, of the measure. Nursery rhymes and the practice of marching illustrate both the sound and the feeling of duple time, respectively.

TRACK 10:
Music in 2/4:
"Song in 2/4" by
J.G. Wilson.

- 6/8 is a compound duple meter. There are six beats per measure. It is counted 1, 2, 3, 4, 5, 6. Yet in faster tempos the first three counts can be counted as 1 and the second three counts can be counted as 2. You will hear the beats 1, 2, 3 when you count 1 and beats 4, 5, 6 when you count 2. In this example, 6/8 is a compound duple meter. However, 6/8 time can also be felt as a triple meter and is used in waltzes.

TRACK 11:
Waltz in 6/8:
"Tristesse" by
P. Cork.

- 3/4 is a simple triple meter. It is counted 1, 2, 3. The 18th-century minuet and the 19th-century waltz are dances that are inseparable from the triple meter to which they are danced.

TRACK 12:
Music in 3/4: *Blue Danube Waltz*, op. 314 by J. Strauss.

- 9/8 is a compound triple meter. It is counted 1-2-3, 4-5-6, 7-8-9.

- 4/4 is a simple quadruple meter. It is counted 1, 2, 3, 4. Common time, or common meter (C or 4/4), as introduced earlier, is formally known as quadruple meter or quadruple time. In each quadruple time signature's four beats, the first beat receives an accent and the third beat receives a secondary accent.

TRACK 13:
Music in 4/4:
"Song in 4/4" by
J.G. Wilson.

- 12/8 is a quadruple compound meter. It is counted 1-2-3, 4-5-6, 7-8-9, 10-11-12.

As stated earlier, there is usually a metrical accent at the beginning of a measure. In duple meter, as in every meter, the accent is usually on the first beat of the measure, giving the first beat a stronger emphasis followed by the second beat's weaker emphasis, the upbeat. Without the metrical accent at the beginning of the measure, it is difficult to discern the meter.

With practice, you can begin to distinguish meter aurally. As an example of duple meter, listen to John Philip Sousa's march "Stars and Stripes Forever." It is in 2/2 meter; the beats are clearly 1-2, 1-2, 1-2, 1-2. As you listen, tap your foot with the beats. Next, listen to Sousa's "Washington Post March." It is in 6/8 meter. When you tap your foot to this march, it is likely that you will tap two beats per measure, as is common when music is written in compound duple meter. But if you listen to the actual notes of the melody, it is easier to hear the six beats in every measure. In "Washington Post March," the 6/8 time signature gives the march a swinging quality. "Stars and Stripes Forever" feels more straightforward.

TRACK 14:
March in cut time: "Stars and Stripes Forever" by John Philip Sousa.

TRACK 15:
March in 6/8: "Washington Post March" by John Philip Sousa.

Behind the Music

John Philip Sousa, America's March King

In addition to serving his country in the Marine band and eventually becoming its director, John Philip Sousa is most famous as a composer of marches. During his career, he also conducted Broadway orchestras, composed operettas, and wrote dance music. His first composition was "Moonlight on the Potomac Waltzes."

From http://upload.wikimedia.org/wikipedia/commons/thumb/3/34/JohnPhilipSousa-Chickering.LOC.jpg/709px-JohnPhilipSousa-Chickering.LOC.jpg

Perhaps for some dancers it is difficult to distinguish between 2/2 or 2/4 and 4/4 meters. Listen to Sousa's cut-time "Stars and Stripes Forever" march. Can you hear the clear 1-2, 1-2, 1-2, 1-2? Next can you hear the 1-2-3-4, 1-2-3-4, 1-2-3-4, 1-2-3-4 in both Jimi Hendrix's "Purple Haze," and Tammy Wynette's "Stand by Your Man," which are in 4/4 meter.

Asymmetrical (Composite) Meter

When a time signature has an odd number of counts and the counts can be grouped in various combinations of twos, threes, or fours within a measure, they are known as asymmetrical or composite. Meters such as 5/4, 7/8, and 11/8 are asymmetrical (or composite). Furthermore, within the beat groupings of 5/4 meter, the beats can be organized conventionally as 1-2, 3-4-5 (the metrical accent and secondary accent are on counts 1 and 3 respectively) or 1-2-3, 4-5 (the metrical accent is on count 1 and the secondary accent is on count 4). In a less conventional manner, the beats could be organized as 1, 2-3, 4-5, thus shifting the measure's secondary accents to counts 2 and 4.

TRACK 16:
Music in 5/4:
"Song in 5/4" by
J.G. Wilson.

Mixed Meter

Mixed meters are measures or groupings of measures in different time signatures. Examples of mixed-meter music date to the Renaissance. Mixed meters also occurred in world music dating to times before the existence of music notation.

TRACK 17:
Music in mixed
meter: "Mixed
Meter Melody"
by J.G. Wilson.

In a mixed-meter composition, the time signature listed at the beginning of a piece of music might be 4/4. Yet, after four measures, the composer changes the time signature to 3/4. After four more measures, the composer returns to 4/4 meter. This changing of meters within a piece of music is referred to as mixed meter. Sting's "Love Is Stronger Than Justice" is an example of the meter changing from the verse, which is in 7/4, to the chorus, which is 4/4.

Say that a composition starts in 5/4. But after two measures, the time signature changes to 3/4 for three measures. This would be counted 1-2-3-4-5, 1-2-3-4-5, 1-2-3, 1-2-3, 1-2-3. Additionally, the first two measures' accents could be organized differently, for example **1**-2-**3**-4-5 or **1**-**2**-3-4-5 (the numbers in bold indicate the metrical accent; the numbers in bold and italics indicate the secondary accent) followed by **1**-2-3, 1-**2**-3, 1-2-**3**. A choreographer might want to count this phrase (a phrase is like a musical sentence) in so-called dancer counts, meaning that he understands the music's meter, yet for the sake of the dancers, he follows the music's meter but adapts the actual counts and accents to a format that is easier for the dancers to follow or remember such as **1**-2-**3**-4-5-**6**-**7**-8-9-10, **1**-2-3-4-**5**-6-7-8-**9**. Once again, it is important that dancers, choreographers, and teachers are aware of music's meter, accents, and stresses. Without this knowledge and awareness, the dancers might sense that they are off the beat or are emphasizing an offbeat or upbeat, when in fact the choreographer has ignored the music's metrical patterns and accents.

Here's another example of a mixed meter. Listen to the song "America" from Leonard Bernstein's *West Side Story* (available on YouTube). Can you hear the 1-2-3-4-5-6, 1 - 2 - 3, 1-2-3-4-5-6, 1 - 2 - 3 ("I want to be in A-mer-i-ca, OK by me in A-mer-i-ca"), the alternating meter? Bernstein, rather than write the time signature change with each measure, notated 6/8 3/4, at the beginning of the song. Throughout the song, the 6/8 measures alternate with 3/4 measures.

Also listen to Debussy's Danse in E (the *Tarantelle styrienne* score is at http://sheetmusicpoint.com/composer/d/debussy/piano/misc/debussy-danse.pdf and you can listen to and watch a performance on the Internet). Can you tell where the music changes meters? Nine measures from the end, the meter becomes 3/4 for four measures and then returns to the original 6/8.

Polymeter

Another type of musical meter is **polymeter**. In a polymeter, different meters occur simultaneously. In Joan Osborne's version of Captain Beefheart's "Right Hand Man," the drums play in 2/4 meter while the guitar and vocal lines proceed in 7/4 (available on YouTube). When the drums join in after the lead guitar's 7/4 meter introduction, the effect of combining the two meters seems to move the measures of seven beats from 1, 3, 5, 7 accents to 2, 4, 6 stresses, creating an overall effect of a 14-count phrase (see chapter 3 to learn about musical phrases). Listen to the instrumental opening of Osborne's "Right Hand Man." Count the drum line. Do you hear the 1-2, 1-2, 1-2, 1-2 of the bass and snare drums? When listening to the guitar rift, can you hear how the 7/4 seems to shift the accents of the drum line?

Note Value

The next illustration shows that there is a simple division of note values. One whole note equals two half notes, one whole note equals four quarter notes, and so forth (see figure 2.4). A simple analogy for the whole note is a whole pie. If the pie is cut in half, there are two halves. If each pie half is cut in half again, the pie is now cut into four pieces, or quarters. A note's actual time value (the time it takes to play the note) varies with the tempo and meter. Tempo refers to how fast or slow the music is played; meter refers to how many beats there are per measure and what kind of note receives one beat. See this chapter's discussions of tempo and meter.

Notice how the consecutive eighth, sixteenth, and thirty-second note stems are connected by thick lines in figure 2.4. These thick lines are called **beams**. Consecutive eighth notes have one beam, sixteenth notes have two beams, and so forth. This connecting of notes in groups is termed **beaming**.

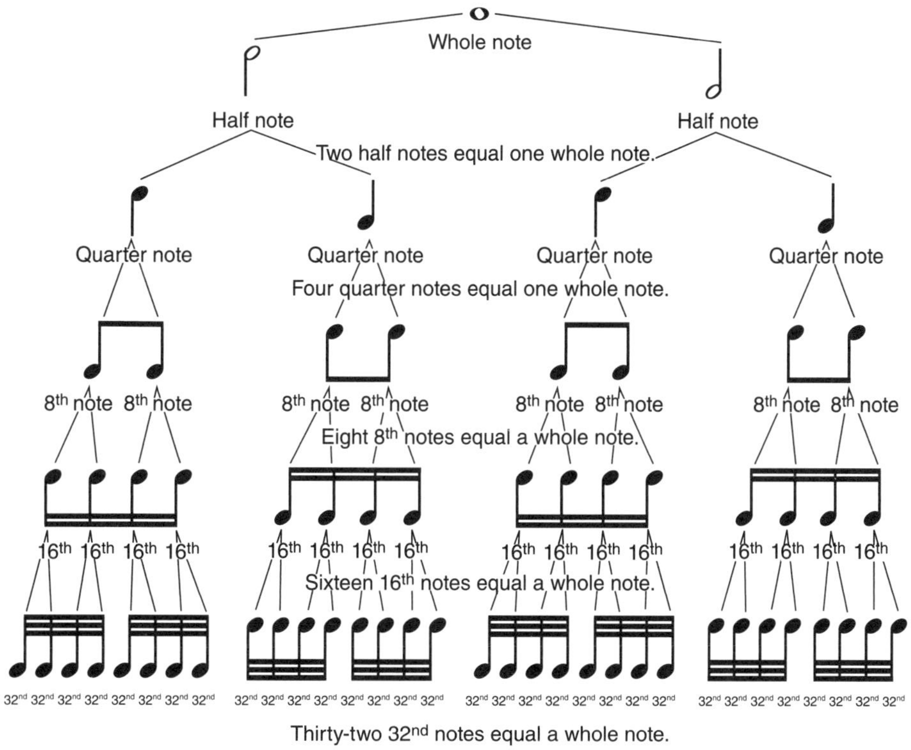
Whole note
Half note
Half note
Two half notes equal one whole note.
Quarter note
Quarter note
Quarter note
Quarter note
Four quarter notes equal one whole note.
8th note 8th note
8th note 8th note
8th note 8th note
8th note 8th note
Eight 8th notes equal a whole note.
16th 16th 16th 16th
16th 16th 16th 16th
16th 16th 16th 16th
16th 16th 16th 16th
Sixteen 16th notes equal a whole note.
32nd 32nd 32nd 32nd 32nd 32nd 32nd 32nd
32nd 32nd 32nd 32nd 32nd 32nd 32nd 32nd
32nd 32nd 32nd 32nd 32nd 32nd 32nd 32nd
32nd 32nd 32nd 32nd 32nd 32nd 32nd 32nd
Thirty-two 32nd notes equal a whole note.

Figure 2.4 Division of a whole note.

Subdivision

TRACK 19: Music in 4/4 with beats subdivided: "Subdivider" by J.G. Wilson.

When a beat is divided into half notes, quarter notes, eighth notes, and so on, it becomes **subdivided**. The number of beats will depend on the specific time signature. How the subdivisions are counted depends on what type of note receives a beat and how much the beat is divided. For example, in 4/4 time, each quarter note receives a beat. If each quarter note were divided, there would be 8 eighth notes as shown in figure 2.4. These eighth notes would be counted 1 & 2 & 3 & 4 &. Dividing the eighth notes into sixteenth notes, which would equal 16 sixteenth notes as shown in figure 2.4, would be counted 1 e & a, 2 e & a, 3 e & a, 4 e & a.

If the time signature were 3/4, one measure of quarter notes would be counted 1, 2, 3. One measure of eighth notes would be counted 1 &, 2 &, 3 &. One measure of sixteenth notes would be counted 1 e & a, 2 e & a, 3 e & a (see figure 2.5).

Moving to a 5/8 time signature, the 5 eighth notes in one measure would be counted 1, 2, 3, 4, 5. Dividing each eighth note into sixteenth notes would result in 10 sixteenth notes that would be counted 1 & 2 & 3 & 4 & 5 & (see figure 2.6).

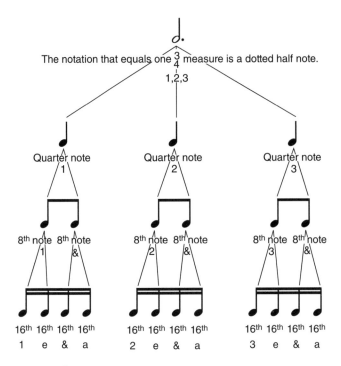

Figure 2.5 Division of notes in 3/4 meter.

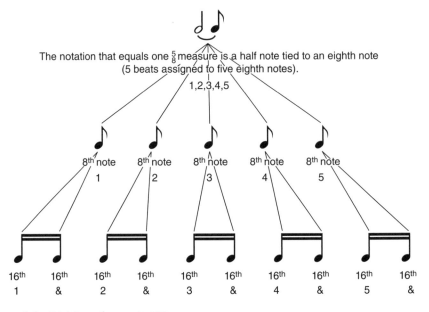

Figure 2.6 Division of notes in 5/8 meter.

Tempo

To know how fast to count the various notes' counts and subdivisions, composers may specify tempos. In both music and dance, **tempo** is an Italian term that describes the rate of speed of the music or the dance (how quickly the beats progress). The following discussion addresses basic terminology and symbols for tempo.

Very often, composers list the tempo they prefer for a composition just above the left end of the first staff of music. Table 2.1 lists some of the most common terms for indicating tempo along with the English translations.

Maelzel's Metronome

Johann Nepomuk Maelzel was a Viennese composer who invented the metronome. His original spring-wound metronome had a sliding weight on an upright pendulum, which connected to a spring (see figure 2.7). Once wound, the spring powered the metronome similarly to a wound wristwatch, a wind-up toy, or a wind-up music box. A chart behind the pendulum showed tempo terminology and numeric speeds. The slowest tempo, largo, or 40 M.M. (Maelzel's metronome), was at the top of the chart. Moving downward, the chart listed progressively faster tempos to presto, or 208 M.M. To play or sing the music at the correct tempo, the music student slid the pendulum's weight to the desired beats per minute (bpm), or tempo term, and freed the pendulum from its restraint. The student then could practice keeping time with the resultant sound, which provided a

TRACK 20: Music in largo: "Pathos" by R. Webb.

TRACK 21: Music in adagio: "A Lonely Tear" by E. Swann.

TRACK 22: Music in moderato: "A Love Nest for Two" by P. Cork.

TRACK 23: Music in allegro: "Bank Holiday" by A.W. Ketelbey.

TRACK 24: Music in presto: "Mayfair Quickstep" by E. Swann.

Table 2.1 Musical Terms Indicating Tempo

Terminology	Definition
largo	very slow, broad
grave	slow, serious
lento (lent)	slow (between largo and adagio)
adagio	slow, leisurely
andante	moderately slow (walking tempo)
moderato	moderate
allegro	fast
vivace	quick, lively
presto	very fast
ad libitum	at liberty; the performers may vary the tempo
a tempo	at the basic or original tempo
rallentando (rall.)	becoming slower
ritardando (rit.)	becoming slower
rubato	flexible tempo

Figure 2.7 A metronome.
© Nola Nolen Holland.

regular pulse at the selected tempo. The purpose of a metronome is threefold: to provide a steady pulse to which a musician may practice, to provide a distinct tempo for those who tend to speed up or slow down as they play or sing, and to provide the tempo at which the composer wishes the music to be performed.

At the beginning of a piece of music, composers may indicate exactly how fast or slowly musicians should play their compositions. They can do this by giving the metronome setting at the beginning of the music next to, or in place of, the tempo marking. As with expression terms or tempo terminology, the metronome settings go above the composition's first staff just after the expression term or tempo terminology. Maelzel's metronome tempos are abbreviated as M.M. and are usually listed inside parentheses. On sheet music or in a musical score, the composer might list a term for the tempo such as poco lento e grazioso followed by the metronome setting (see figure 2.8*a*). Alternatively, the composer may give only the type of note that receives one beat, the equal sign, and then the number of beats per minute (see figure 2.8*b*).

a M.M. ♩ = 72   *b* ♪ = 112-132

Figure 2.8 *(a)* This notation indicates that there should be 72 beats per minute with the quarter note receiving one beat and *(b)* this particular indication shows a tempo range of 112 to 132 beats per minute with an eighth note receiving one beat.

Modern Digital Metronomes

A music student may practice keeping time or staying in time with an electronic or digital metronome's beats, which provide steady, regular beats at the selected tempo. Again, the purpose of a metronome is to provide a consistent pulse to which a musician may practice. Today's digital metronomes provide a sound for each beat. Some even provide a flashing light for each beat. Cell phone users may even be able to download a metronome application. In computer music composition programs, the metronome sound often delineates each measure's count 1 with a unique sound and may also be enabled or disabled as composers create or play back their compositions.

Rhythm

Rhythm is a combination of long and short sounds. These long and short sounds exist within the meter of a piece of music. Combining or dividing beats creates rhythm. Rhythm is related to, yet different from, the beat of the music. Rhythm is supported by the elements of beat and meter but can be an entity unto itself. Rhythm can distinguish and contribute to the significance of a melody. The rhythm or the beat of a piece of music can also inspire you to move to or choreograph to specific music. Dancers often confuse rhythm with beat. To understand rhythm, you must first understand the elements of rhythm.

To indicate various rhythms within a measure or beyond a measure, composers use various notations. Combinations of notes and rests define some rhythms that may also exist within a measure or even a beat. They may also extend beyond a measure. Ties lengthen some notes, which lengthen the playing of a pitch, while other notes may be followed by a dot, which increases a note's value by half.

Dot

The **dot** lengthens the value of a note or rest by half of the note's or rest's value. For example, a dot placed after a half note extends the half note's value as if it were tied to a quarter note, as shown in figure 2.9. Similarly, a dot following a quarter rest is equivalent to the quarter rest plus an eighth rest as shown in figure 2.10. The tie combines two notes' values and can also extend the note and affects rhythm into the following measure.

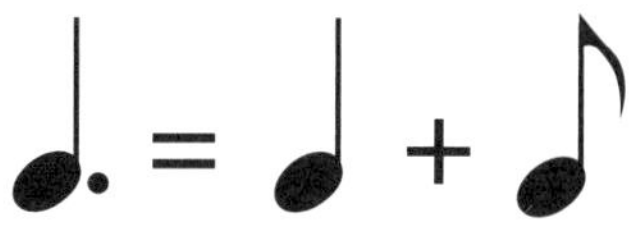

Figure 2.9   Dotted quarter note.

Figure 2.10   Dotted quarter rest.

Tie

A **tie** is a curved line connecting, but not touching, two notes of the same pitch. It indicates that a pitch should be held for the combined value of the two notes. A tie may link notes within the same measure so that the notes' values are combined within the measure. It may also extend the duration of a note to one in the following measure, as in the examples in figure 2.11. Interestingly, ties do not apply to rests. Figure 2.11 shows notes that are tied together across bar lines. See the bass staff in figure 1.18 for notes that are tied together within a measure.

Figure 2.11 Ties extending a note's time value into the following measure.

Triplet

When three notes play in the time of two notes of the same value or in the time value of one note of the next larger value, they are a **triplet**. Figure 2.12 gives some examples of triplets. Listen to a recording of Cole Porter's "Night and Day" online. Can you hear the triplets for the lyrics "you are the" and "un-der the"? In the cut-time refrain, Porter has the triplets fit in the time of one count.

There are also instances of 5, 7, 13, or more notes played in the time of 1 note, as seen in figure 2.13.

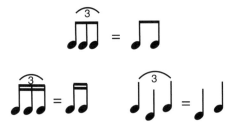

Figure 2.12 Example of triplets.

Figure 2.13 A grouping of 7 sixteenth notes played in the time of 1 beat in 3/4 meter.
Reprinted from F. Chopin, 1836, Polonaise, Op. 26, No. 1 in C sharp minor. In *Everybody's favorite Chopin album*, No. 56, edited by Samuel Spivak (New York: Amsco Music Publishing Co).

$\mathcal{B}$ehind the $\mathcal{M}$usic

Cole Porter and Fred Astaire

Cole Porter composed the song "Night and Day" for the 1932 Broadway production *Gay Divorce*, Fred Astaire's final Broadway show. In 1934 Astaire and Ginger Rogers danced and sang the song in the film *The Gay Divorcee*.

A triplet in dance is usually referring to triple meter (e.g., 3/4) rather than the dancer's steps following an actual musical triplet note for note. Dance teachers and their students often follow the music's beat rather a melody's note values as in performing balancés or waltz steps. It is possible for dancers to dance to each note or each beat's subdivision in a triplet, yet choreography where the movements follow each note or beat might be derided as music visualization.

Syncopation

Syncopation occurs within a measure when a weak beat receives emphasis. This means that when the second or fourth beat in a measure of 4/4 meter receives emphasis, the music is syncopated. Normally the first beat of a measure receives the strongest emphasis and the third beat of the measure receives a secondary accent, so syncopation creates offbeat accents through the use of rests, ties, various note combinations, dotted notes, accents, and dynamic signs (see figure 2.14).

TRACK 25:
Music with simple syncopation: "Fascination Rag" by P. Cork.

TRACK 26:
Music with complex syncopation: "Smooth Work" by E. Thomas.

Syncopation is the norm for jazz and Latin music and the many styles of African music and its offshoots. However, Western music's classical concertos and symphonies as well as world folk songs and popular songs also contain abundant examples of syncopation. Some popular music examples are in Frank Sinatra's rendition of Coleman and Leigh's "The Best Is Yet to Come," George Harrison's "Something," Sheryl Crow's "All I Wanna Do," the Cranberries' "Zombie," and Gillian Welch's "Didn't Leave Nobody but the Baby" (all available on the Internet). Because of its unexpected offbeat nature, syncopation can lend variety, excitement, humor, and flavor to music.

Syncopation in Jazz Dance and Latin Dance

The accents and patterns of a rhythm often influence dance. Jazz dance, for example, has characteristics of sharply accented movements originally inspired by the offbeat accents of jazz music. Today jazz dance continues to evolve through the influence of rap and hip-hop music. In Latin social dance, the rhythms of the accompanying Latin music distinguish one style from another. Latin dances and their accompanying music even share the same names, such as mambo, tango, samba, rumba, and merengue. These dances with their distinctive rhythmic patterns have abundant examples of syncopation.

Polyrhythm

When different percussion instruments play different rhythms simultaneously, the texture of the simultaneous rhythms is called polyrhythm. Several examples of polyrhythms occur in traditional African, Asian, and Latin American music. Polyrhythms occur when several drummers play several different types of drums simultaneously. Each drum not only has a unique sound but also "speaks" a unique rhythm that often directs the dancers' steps and movements. African music, for example, is renowned for its multiple layers of rhythm, complex syncopation, and drumming that directs the dancers' movements.

Figure 2.14 Types of notated syncopation. *(a)* Syncopation by use of rests, *(b)* syncopation by use of ties, *(c)* syncopation by use of note combination, *(d)* syncopation by use of dotted notes, *(e)* syncopation by use of accents, and *(f)* syncopation by use of dynamic symbols.

(b) Reprinted, by permission, from Alfred Publishing. ©1970 Warner Bros. Corp.

Summary

As a dancer, you should be able to distinguish between beat and rhythm. Beyond this basic point, your training and orientation in a particular movement style—such as flamenco, jazz dance, tap dance, character dance, or African dance—will significantly influence your response to the element of musical time and rhythm.

In modern dance, the element of time has several aspects as well, such as speed, rhythm, pulse, breath, accent, and beat. The most basic dance element of time is speed (tempo), how fast to dance. How to count the music is often a secondary consideration. You need to know whether to count in twos, threes, fours, fives, sixes, sevens, eights, or any other numeric combination and configuration (such as asymmetrical meters and mixed meters). Tempo distinctions and counting music are critical to your ability to perform to complex music and critical to a choreographer's ability to understand and create movement to complex music. As a class dances the instructor's exercises or student-created movements, do the dancers follow the beat of the music? Or do they move with or in contrast to the rhythm that occurs as an additional temporal (i.e., time-related) layer of the music? Do the dancers follow their internal rhythms with no music at all? Dancers, choreographers, and teachers need to know these distinctions in order to dance or create movement for performances or classes.

Discerning meter without looking at the written music requires extensive experience in aural analysis. Some dancers find it very difficult to discern 2/4 from 4/4 unless they know how to listen for accents that establish the first beat and secondary accents in a 4/4 meter. Familiarity with and appreciation for syncopation help tap, jazz, and flamenco dancers perform basic movements of their chosen genres with clarity and accuracy.

For a choreographer, looking at a music score with a metronome listing can give an approximate idea of how fast the music is. For a dance teacher, knowing the basics of musical time allows them to educate students about music as a vital component of a dance class. By practicing the exercises at the end of the chapter, you will better understand beat, meter, tempo, rhythm, syncopation, and polyrhythm.

Practical Applications

Supplementary Exercises, Activities, and Projects

1. Beat: In a dance studio, select a meter and practice walking with a steady beat. Apply a metrical accent to the first beat of each measure of the meter and a secondary accent to another beat. (In 4/4 meter, the secondary accent is the third beat; in 6/8 meter, it is the fourth beat.) For a follow-up activity, accent the weak beats, choosing, for example, the second or fourth beat of each measure if walking in 4/4 meter. Finally, combine the usual metrically accented measures with measures in which the weak beats are stressed to create phrases with changing accented and stressed beats. Work in groups to create various walking patterns by combining the usually accented measures with the measures where you have accented the weak beats. Remember to work only with the beats. Do not divide the beats yet. Perform each group's accented pattern separately for the class and then perform some of the patterns simultaneously. Is this difficult to do? Why?

   Next, evenly divide the meter's beats in half and create an eighth-note pattern of 1 & 2 & 3 & 4 & that emphasizes the usual accents: the strong accent on 1 and the weaker accent on 3. Divide the eighth notes in half, creating a sixteenth-note pattern, which musicians count as such: 1 e & a, 2 e & a, 3 e & a, 4 e & a. What happens when you try (or the class tries) to walk on each of these subdivisions of the beats? Did you feel the need to jog or run in order to move with each note?

2. Meter: Listen to several short pieces of music selected by your instructor. Identify the meters by listening to the examples. As a class, decide how you would count the music. Is the music in twos, threes, fours, or fives? Hint: Try to discover the meter by finding the accent of count 1. In a waltz, for example, notice the three-beat grouping with a strong accent on the first beat of the three notes. Listen to one of John Philip Sousa's marches written in 6/8. How does the class want to count it? According to the music, how should it be counted? Listen to Handel's Sarabande in D Minor. It also has beat groupings of three. But the stress is on the second beat. How can you find the first beat of the measure in the sarabande? A meter of five is an asymmetrical meter. How are "Sunset Boulevard" and the "Theme From Mission Impossible" different from the previous examples? Count each music example out loud in class. (Performance samples are available online.)

3. Rhythm: After discussing beat in class and completing exercises 1 and 2, create a phrase of rhythm. Before creating the rhythm, determine the meter. Practice clapping the meter at first. Then create the rhythm. At the next class meeting, perform your rhythmic phrase by clapping or drumming. The instructor can guide you and your classmates to play your phrases in sequences as well as combine your phrases in simultaneous performances, thereby creating polyrhythms. To coordinate the rhythms, the instructor should determine the length of the phrases (perhaps one measure initially, then two measures, four measures, and so on).

4. Syncopation: Listen to a waltz and a march. Are there places in the music that have syncopation? Then listen to jazz music. Is it possible to detect the syncopation in the jazz excerpt? Does syncopation occur throughout the jazz example? Next, listen to world music. How does it compare to the other excerpts you have heard? In world music, try to locate examples from Africa, the Caribbean, Latin America, and Asia. Listen to samples from cultures that prominently feature syncopation in their music.

For additional assignments, handouts, web links, and more, please visit the web resource at www. HumanKinetics.com/MusicFundamentalsForDance.

Elements
of Melody

3

A pretty girl is like a melody
That haunts you night and day,
Just like the strain of a haunting refrain,
She'll start up-on a marathon
And run around your brain.
You can't escape she's in your memory.
By morning night and noon.
She will leave you and then come back again,
A pretty girl is just like a pretty tune.

Irving Berlin,
American composer and lyricist (1888-1989)

When you think of melody, a beautiful song might come to mind. Or perhaps an exciting theme from a movie sparks creative juices. But why study melodies? Construction and development of melodies resemble construction and development of solo dances as well as a soloist's dance among other dancers. Understanding melodic construction lends knowledge to dance composition and renders you better able to select music for composition and choreography. It makes you a better listener and analyst and, in the end, a better dancer, choreographer, and teacher.

A **melody** is a sequence of related pitches. Melody is the dominant part of the music that people hear in popular songs. It is the part of the music that a solo singer sings; it is the tune. Melody helps people to remember or recall music. It is the signature of the music much like a repeated or outstanding phrase of movements can be the signature of a dance.

Two Types of Melody

TRACK 27:
Music with
self-contained
melody: "Self
Contained" by
J.G. Wilson.

There are two basic categories of melodies. One type is self-contained, which includes songs or short instrumental pieces that are complete in themselves (Seigmeister 1965). Most popular songs on the radio and tunes that you have on your phone or portable music device are self-contained. These songs usually have a primary melody, a chorus (refrain), and sometimes a bridge (a short transitional section that leads to a secondary melody). The second type of melody is open ended; these are works that contain more melodic development than self-contained melodies. A melody with an open end means that the ending of the tune gives an impression that more music will follow. Of course, there are also themes in sonatas and symphonies that are complete in themselves and that can stand alone as melodies as well as open-ended themes that lead into subsequent development sections or to subsequent themes.

The 1928 song "I'd Rather Be Blue Over You" by Fred Fisher and Billy Rose includes several open-ended melodies (both the song and its lyrics can be found online). At the end of the song's third phrase ("Than be happy with somebody else"), the pitch for the word *else* is not the song's key center pitch, which creates the sense that the song is not over. The open ending of the secondary melody (beginning with the lyrics "I'm crazy about ya") leads into the third melodic line ("I need a little ah, little ooh"). After this third melody's open ending, the song returns to the opening melody before beginning the song's conclusion.

Claude Debussy's *Clair de lune* (1888) provides an example of open-ended melodies within an instrumental composition (the piano score and recordings can be found online). The end of the first melody in measure 14 leads into the second melody in measure 15 which in turn ends with arpeggios in measures 25 and 26 that introduce the third melody in measure 27. There is a variation on the third melody which acts as a transitional section (beginning at measure 43) and leads to the return of the first melody in measure 51.

TRACK 28: Debussy's *Clair de lune* has open-ended melodies.

Many characteristics are common in both self-contained and open-ended melodies. A melody will be in a specific key and will have rhythmic structure, a climax, and intervals between the pitches of the melody. This chapter investigates the basic melodic characteristics of range, shape, and movement.

Range

Range is made up of the melody's highest and lowest pitches. When the term *range* is applied to a melody, it refers to the distance from the lowest note to the highest. Melodies with a narrow range of movement may suggest a mood of quiet, calm, or stillness. A wide melodic range may give the impression of freedom or more expansiveness. Songs such as Arlen and Harburg's "Somewhere Over the Rainbow" and Tormé and Wells' "The Christmas Song" ("Chestnuts roasting on an open fire . . .") have melodic intervals of an octave, a wide range.

As a dancer can perform at high levels or low, melodic range refers to the distance between the lowest note to the highest.

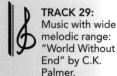

TRACK 29:
Music with wide melodic range: "World Without End" by C.K. Palmer.

TRACK 30:
Music with narrow melodic range: the "Ode to Joy" theme from the fourth movement of Beethoven's Ninth Symphony.

A wider melodic range can also be more jarring or create enjoyable music depending on the intent of the composer. For example, the opening rhythm and lead guitar riffs in Jimi Hendrix's "Purple Haze" display a wider (and dissonant) melodic range. The melodic range in Rodgers and Hammerstein's "Bali Hai" begins with a wide melodic interval that evokes the enchanting essence of a tropical paradise. Antonio Carlos Jobim and Gene Lees' haunting bossa nova "Corcovado" ("Quiet Nights of Quiet Stars") exemplifies a narrow melodic range, as does the French folk song "Frère Jacques" ("Are You Sleeping?").

Shape

Shape is the contour of the melody's pitches. For instance, melodies with the contour of an arch may have pitches close together, far apart, or a combination of both. Music scholars describe the shape of melodies as being curves (contours) or lines. Melodic shape can be compared to connecting the dots in a children's activity book, then smoothing out the contour. Melodic lines provide upward, downward, and overall motion in a melody. The pitches of a melody may move upward or downward and could even be applied to creating a graph that shows ascending or descending lines, arches, or even waves.

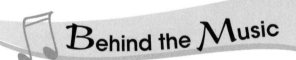

Behind the Music

Rodgers and Hammerstein: Establishing Dance as an Equal Artistic Component in Musicals

Richard Rodgers (1902-1979) and Oscar Hammerstein (1895-1960) were a famous composer–lyricist duo in 20th-century musical theater. *Oklahoma* (1943) was their first collaboration. Agnes de Mille's choreography for *Oklahoma* set a new standard for dance in stage productions. Rodgers and Hammerstein continued to include dance scenes in their ensuing collaborations. *State Fair* (1944) has dance scenes set in the Starlight Dance Meadow on the fairgrounds. *Carousel* (1945) features "Louise's Ballet," a dance scene similar in concept to *Oklahoma*'s "Dream Ballet." *South Pacific* (1949) presents the hilarious "Thanksgiving Follies." *The King and I* (1951) includes dance in the "Small House of Uncle Thomas" and the "Shall We Dance" scenes. The 1965 film version of *The Sound of Music* (1959) featured a version of the ländler, an Austrian social dance in 3/4 meter.

These melodic shapes of lines, curves, and waves can be combined in infinite ways. Furthermore, music scholars can become very involved in the analysis of melodies, melodic lines, curves, and their various combinations, especially with the influences of rhythmic structure, climaxes, and modes. Dancers, teachers, and choreographers need to know the basics of melodic shape and be able to discern a melody's ascending or descending line, its curves or waves, and the presence of combinations of melodic shapes so that they may discern the climax of each phrase and how the phrases relate to those around it.

Listen to George Bruns' "Scales and Arpeggios" from the 1970 Disney animated film *The Aristocats*. The melody is composed of ascending and descending lines and waves. The melodic lines in this particular song are the **scales**. As described in chapter 1, scales are the pitches of a key played in an ascending or descending sequence, usually progressing by steps and half steps. The first pitch of a scale is called the **tonic** pitch which is also the pitch that names the key. The melodic waves in "Scales and Arpeggios" are the **arpeggios**, an Italian musical term for when the notes of a chord are played sequentially.

Movement

Movement, or the motion of a piece, is how quickly the rhythm of the melody combines or divides the notes. The term *movement* can be an overall concept when applied to a melody or a descriptor of the type of melody as mentioned in the previous section on melodic shape. As in dance movement, where large movements such as jumps and partnered overhead lifts often require more time to prepare for and execute the movements, melody is similar. When a melody has greater melodic range (larger movement), it may also have more energy. Generally, when the melodic range is smaller, the melody may seem smoother and calmer. Of course, there are musical examples that contradict these statements, such as Rimsky-Korsakov's "Flight of the Bumble Bee," which moves in half steps with a small range and great energy.

In melodic movement, there are rhythmic and tonal aspects as well. Rhythmically, when a melody is presented in smaller, or subdivided, units of time, the listener perceives the melody as having forward motion. A modern example of subdivided melodic time is in the verses of Fiona Apple's "Extraordinary Machine." When units of time are combined into longer spans of time, the melody seems slowed. Duke Ellington and his clarinetist Barney Bigard did this very thing (used longer note values and tied notes) in the hauntingly beautiful first section of "Mood Indigo." Most melodies are a combination of longer and shorter note values creating rhythms that contribute to the effect of the speed of the melody.

With regard to the tonal aspect of movement, melodies are generally categorized as either conjunct or disjunct. **Conjunct melodies** move in steps, whereas **disjunct melodies** move by leaps between the notes of the melody. These two types of movement are apparent in the penultimate phrase of "The Star Spangled Banner." The notes corresponding with the lyrics "o'er the land of the free" are conjunct. The opening phrases of the song ("O say can you see by the dawn's early light, what so proudly we hailed at the twilight's last gleaming?") definitely contain disjunct movement. On the other hand, Rodgers and Hammerstein's "Do-Re-Mi" epitomizes conjunct movement as the melody moves up and down the scale in steps. Another example of disjunct movement is in Adolph Adam's "O Holy Night." This melody is composed of thirds, fourths, and larger intervals (the distance between two notes); therefore, it has a more disjunct motion. Conjunct and disjunct movement concepts help to create the emotional quality of a melody. However, conjunct and disjunct movements, or a combination of the two movement types, do not always produce the same emotional qualities. Melodic movement combined with the tonal elements of range and shape plus the rhythmic subdivision or combination of time define and distinguish one melody from another.

Melodic Structure

Motives, climaxes, and cadences are elements of **melodic structure**. In a larger sense, music's structure defines its form. The same is true in dance. Analyzing a musical composition or a dance work yields insight into the choices the composer or choreographer made regarding the composition's overall concept and reveals the work's compositional devices. These musical or dance structures are essential knowledge for any composer, choreographer, or teacher. By being able to understand music's structure and, more specifically, a melody's structure, a choreographer can link movement dynamics to the melody's dynamics, thus avoiding incongruencies between music and choreography such as ignoring the melody's or the theme's climactic moments or having a blank stage at the most powerful moment in the music.

Melodic Motive

The **motive** (a short group of notes arranged in a distinctive pattern or design) is a primary element of melodic structure. Motives are also elements of a phrase, a longer melodic statement (see also the section titled Phrase). Motives may be as short as two pitches or as long as a few measures. A composer will build upon, alter, and manipulate a motive in many ways in order to develop it, perhaps expanding it into a phrase, melody, or theme. Motives are developed and usually classified as melodic, rhythmic, or a combination of the two.

Composers first state the motive, then usually repeat it. If the motive is not repeated exactly, it may be altered melodically or rhythmically. When a motive is repeated beginning on different (usually successive) pitches, the repetition creates what is referred to as a **melodic sequence**. This sequencing of the motive usually alters the harmony and melody as well and often occurs in a developed work, a longer composition with sections and a specific form. Additionally, a motive needs to be repeated only once to be considered a sequence. A **sequence**, therefore, is a motive pattern repeated on a different pitch. Although not in a developed work, one well-known example of a motive sequence is in the refrain or chorus of the traditional French Christmas carol

TRACK 31: Music with motivic sequences: the first movement from Beethoven's Fifth Symphony.

"Angels We Have Heard on High." After the first statement of the motive with the lyric "Glo-o-o-o-o-o-o-ria," the melodic motive descends a step or a half step (respectively within the major mode) with the subsequent two repeats of "Gloria," creating a melodic sequence.

A melodic motive can be quite memorable. The two opening pitches of Lennon and McCartney's "Hey Jude" are a great example of a melodic motive. If you are familiar with this song, you need only hear the first two notes of the song to know what will follow. An example of a melodic repetition through motive sequences followed by a different melodic motive being repeated twice verbatim is in Frank Churchill's "Some Day My Prince Will Come" from the 1937 Disney animated movie *Snow White and the Seven Dwarfs*.

Rhythmic Motive

A **rhythmic motive** is a short sequence of sounds or pitches based more on a distinct rhythm than the melody. In Maurice Ravel's *Bolero*, which he originally composed as a ballet, the rhythmic motive begins and continues throughout the work. Listen also to Steve Reich's *Music for Large Ensemble* (1978), which opens with repeated and layered rhythmic motives played on the piano, xylophone, flutes, and marimba.

Melodic-Rhythmic Motive

The **melodic-rhythmic** motive is the most common type of motive. As evidenced by its name, this type of motive is a combination of rhythmic and melodic features. Duke Ellington's "C-Jam Blues" provides a shorter example

Behind the Music

Ravel's Ballet *Bolero*

French composer Maurice Ravel (1875-1937) composed *Bolero* (1928) as a ballet for Ida Rubenstein's (1885-1960) dance company. It premiered in Paris with choreography by Bronislava Nijinska (1891-1972). Because of the score's popularity, the music quickly transitioned into standard orchestral repertoire. Ravel was actually surprised by the composition's popularity because it was based on simple musical concepts. He constructed *Bolero* with a constantly repeating rhythmic ostinato as well as alternating and repeating melodic themes that sound varied because Ravel kept changing the instrumentation and built the tension of the repetition to a loud ending climax. In 1989, choreographer Lar Lubovich created a duet set to *Bolero* titled *Fandango*, which is also the musical style of Ravel's *Bolero* and was originally the title of Ravel's ballet score.

of a rhythmic and melodic motive that is similar in both rhythmic and melodic aspects to Beethoven's motive for the first movement of his Fifth Symphony. In listening to the first movement of this symphony, you will hear the motive repeated many times with several variations. One difference between the motive in Ellington's "C-Jam Blues" and the motive in the first movement of Beethoven's Fifth Symphony is that Ellington's ascends and Beethoven's descends. See this chapter's web resource for extended learning activities that will develop your skill at identifying various motives.

Dance Motif

Knowledge of musical motives is useful in creating dance movement. The term for motive in dance is *motif*. Having one movement (or motif) and then adding to it, as in Trisha Brown's compositional technique of accumulation (dancing a movement, then dancing that movement and another, then dancing those two and adding a third, and so on), or expanding a movement motif through augmentation (lengthening the time it takes to execute each movement of a phrase by slowing the performance of the movements) offers many options for creating dance technique combinations or dance composition phrases respectively as well as phrases for dance works.

Melodic Phrase

TRACK 32:
Music with melodic phrases: the American folk tune, "Yankee Doodle."

A **phrase** in music can be compared to a sentence. In language, a phrase is a component of a sentence, is a fragment of the sentence, and may or may not be a complete thought. In music, a phrase is a component of melody and can be a complete musical thought. Many folk and popular tunes consist of four phrases set to a four-line poem. "Yankee Doodle" is such an example of a four-line poem set to four phrases of music. Each phrase in "Yankee Doodle" is four measures long. In fact, the most common phrase length is four measures. See this chapter's web resources for extended learning activities that will help you develop your skill at identifying various phrase lengths as well as motives that are used as building blocks of melodic phrases.

Cadence of a Melodic Phrase

The ending of a musical phrase is called a **cadence**. Not to be confused with a drum corps' repeated rhythmic phrases or the drumming of a marching band's percussion section, cadence in the structure of a melody is where the phrase rests momentarily or comes to a stopping point. Cadences divide music into phrases. A melodic phrase may end with an incomplete cadence or a complete cadence. The alternative terminology for incomplete cadence is inconclusive cadence. The complete cadence is also known as a perfect cadence. Regardless of the terminology or type, cadence determines a phrase's conclusion. If the cadence gives the listener a sense that more music will follow, it is an **incom-**

plete cadence. If the cadence gives the listener the sense that the phrase has ended, it is a **complete cadence**.

In the Scottish folk tune "My Bonnie Lies Over the Ocean," every fourth measure has a moment of rest marked by a quarter rest. The quarter rest, therefore, marks the cadence. Even if you are not familiar with the song, you should be able to see the quarter rests and read the lines of the verse to sense the ending of each verse's phrase in "My Bonnie" (see figure 3.1).

The incomplete cadence in a melody usually ends on a note other than the tonic. The **tonic** pitch is the first and last pitch of a scale. The illustration of "My Bonnie" is in the key of C. The first three phrases of "My Bonnie," as shown previously, end with incomplete cadences; they end on a pitch other than the tonic C, giving the listener the feeling that more music will follow after the end of each phrase and that the song is not yet complete. The last phrase, "Oh, bring back my Bonnie to me," ends with a complete cadence because it ends on the pitch of C, the tonic pitch. That ending of the phrase on the pitch of C gives the fourth phrase a sense of conclusion. For the ultimate example of a work-ending cadence, listen to Manuel de Falla's "Ritual Fire Dance" from his ballet *El Amor Brujo* (*Love the Magician*).

Phrase-ending effects in dance are similar to cadences in music but are indicated through the body's position, the dancer's focus, or the dance's correspondence to or independence from the musical phrase. Because dance is often tied to its accompanying music, the music may set the phrasing of the dance. Conversely, some dances begin before the music starts and end after the music ends. Obviously, they are not completely tied to the music. Yet, in an effort not to be too heavily influenced by music, choreographers sometimes create movement independently of the music in order to establish contrasting

My Bonnie Lies Over the Ocean

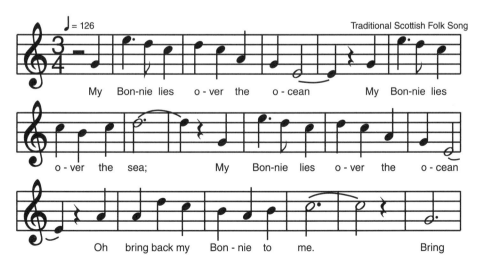

Figure 3.1 Music and lyrics for the first verse of "My Bonnie Lies Over the Ocean."
Adapted from T. Raph, *The American song treasury.*

phrases or to create a movement counterpoint to the music. Equally important for dance teachers is creating movement phrasing that is independent of or linked to the phrasing of music. Training dancers to be aware of phrasing is an essential aspect of dance education.

Melody, harmony, and rhythm are the three elements of cadence. Where the melody is or what it has been doing leading up to the cadence, what pitch is employed at the cadence, and how the pitches are subdivided or combined while leading to the cadence determine the incomplete or complete cadence. These three elements function together to produce an emphasis, a temporary pause, or the culmination of a musical idea. Generally, the cadence serves as the goal in each phrase toward which all of the tones move.

Climax of a Melodic Phrase

TRACK 33: Adagio from the "Grand Pas de Deux" from Tchaikovsky's *The Nutcracker*. This piece has obvious climaxes in its melodic phrases.

The climax of a melody is the point where the intensity of the phrase reaches a peak. The climax is often the highest pitch of a melody, a place in the music with a dramatic increase or decrease in dynamics, or one where tension has been created through the use of intervals. Returning to the example of "The Star Spangled Banner," in the penultimate phrase of the song, "O'er the land of the free," the pitch that corresponds with the word *free* is the climax of the entire song and may also be the loudest point of the song. The last phrase, "and the home of the brave," ends on the tonic pitch. All of the melodic phrases have built toward the climactic pitch of the word *free* in the anthem. Similarly, operatic arias often build to a climaxing high pitch. Examples of climaxing pitches abound in arias by Monteverdi, Mozart, Verdi, Puccini, and Rossini.

Phrases without climax could eventually become very boring listening. A melody would be difficult to distinguish and would not have a focal point. In the resulting climax-less music, listeners might be confused and have difficulty remembering the melody even if they were making an effort to do so.

The climax of a musical phrase can be echoed visually through choreography.

Theme

A primary melody in a longer composition is called a **theme**. Just as motives are elements of melodies, themes are melodic elements of larger and longer musical works. Themes are longer melodies that may contain motives as previously referred to in the first movement of Beethoven's Fifth Symphony. Many longer musical works have at least two themes, an A theme and a B theme. Symphonies often have A-theme groups, B-theme groups, and sometimes more. Just as manipulation expands the motive into a melody, a composer manipulates themes to develop a work into a longer piece of music. Similar to the theme of a written composition, a musical theme expresses a main idea, a musical thought. It may also express or exemplify an emotion or a mood.

Contrapuntal Theme

A **contrapuntal theme,** or a theme where counterpoint occurs, happens when one or more themes play or blend at the same time. As an initial but not orchestral example, Meredith Willson famously juxtaposed the melodies of his tune "Pick a Little, Talk a Little" with Edwin P. Christy's 19th-century tune "Good Night Ladies" in *The Music Man*, creating a **quodlibet**, the simultaneous performance of well-known tunes. Likewise, in orchestral works, developing the theme's melodic material may also result in a contrapuntal theme. This means that as a composer expands a theme, he may choose to have different versions of the theme played simultaneously. Beethoven and many other classical composers developed symphonic, concerto, or sonata themes and the resultant movements (movements are distinct sections of longer musical works) by giving the theme a contrapuntal treatment so that versions of a melody or motive occur simultaneously.

Contrapuntal treatment of a motive or melody may employ one of two types of counterpoint: imitative counterpoint or nonimitative counterpoint. Some imitative counterpoint devices that a composer may use to create contrapuntal

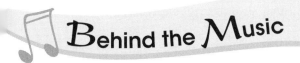

Behind the Music

Beethoven and Dance

Although most famous for his symphonies, Beethoven also composed two ballets, *Muzik zu einem Ritterballett* (*Music for a Knight's Ballet*, 1791) and *Die Geschöpfe des Prometheus* (*The Creatures of Prometheus*, 1801), as well as sets of minuets, waltzes, and contradances.

treatments, particularly in a fugue (an imitative, multivoice composition), are inversion, retrograde, retrograde inversion, augmentation, and diminution. **Imitative counterpoint** includes canons and rounds in which groups of instruments or voices repeat the melody at specific overlapping time intervals. Inversion occurs when a melody moves in the opposite direction of its original statement. In retrograde counterpoint, a melody moves backward from the last pitch to the first. Retrograde inversion means that the melody moves in the opposite direction but also backward. Augmentation lengthens a melody's note values, and diminution shortens a melody's note values. In **nonimitative counterpoint**, simultaneously occurring melodies do not have to coincide or match in rhythm, time, or key. They merely occur simultaneously. See chapter 4 for further discussion of contrapuntal devices.

Thematic Development

As stated previously, many of the devices that develop a motive can also develop the theme of a longer musical work. Thematic development expands a theme. Lengthening of a theme may occur in two general ways. The previously discussed contrapuntal treatments are one way. A theme may also be varied repeatedly, which is known as thematic variation.

Forms of thematic variation date to ancient times and have two basic types: sectional and continuous. In sectional variations, also called theme and variations or variations on a theme, pauses separate each variation, which allow a listener to easily discern each variation's ending. Romantic-era (1790-1910) composer Frédéric Chopin (1810-1849) created five sectional variations, each separated by an orchestral **ritornello** (a short repeated section that he also varies) in his Variations in B-Flat, op. 2, which is based on Mozart's "Là ci darem la mano" ("There We Will Entwine Our Hands") from his opera *Don Giovanni* (*Don Juan*, 1787). In his "Variationen über ein Thema von Rossini" (Variations on a Theme by Rossini), Chopin created continuous variations using one of Rossini's opera themes, "Non più mesta" ("No Longer Sad") from *La Cenerentola* (*Cinderella*, 1817). Continuous variations have no pauses between the variations. As a variation ends, the next begins.

Choreography can also use these same motive, melodic, or thematic techniques. These techniques may apply to the development of phrases or entire works. In teaching, the theories of motive, motive development, theme, contrapuntal devices, and theme variation techniques apply to creating and developing class exercises for students' technical levels as well. These devices can further develop students' technical skills by using the same idea for an exercise but expanding and extending it at a more advanced level by varying the speed, sequence, meter, and phrasing. Development of a musical idea, choreographic idea, or dance movement exercise, however, is totally dependent on the craftsmanship and talent of the composer, choreographer, or dance teacher, respectively.

Summary

Melody in music is much more than a tune one hums along with while listening to music or upon leaving a concert. It is a well-crafted element of a song or musical composition. Similarly, whether a choreographer is creating a dance solo or a dance work for a soloist with a group, or whether a teacher is creating a phrase for a dance class, it is helpful for dancers and teachers alike to know how movement can relate to or be influenced by melodic structure.

This chapter has covered the various types of melody, melodic characteristics, and melodic structure. Chapter 4, Texture, relates to music and can also relate to the texture of a dance work. Before moving forward, however, you should complete the exercises and experiences offered at the end of this chapter in order to gain a practical understanding of melody.

Practical Applications

Supplementary Exercises, Activities, and Projects

1. Range, shape, movement, cadence, and climax: As a class, listen to various melodic examples. While listening to each example, determine the range, shape, movement, cadence, and climaxes of the phrases of the melodies. Is there one phrase that seems more important than all of the others? If so, this is the climax of the melody. Begin with the examples listed in the chapter or listen to instructor-selected examples.

2. Structure: In class, listen to various melodies to determine their structure. Listen for motives (melodic, rhythmic, or melodic and rhythmic) and phrases. Listen to popular songs and determine their melodic structure. What is the relationship between the lyrics and the melody?

3. Thematic analysis: In class, listen to a movement of a classical music sonata, quartet, quintet, or symphony. As a group, determine the theme, when it begins, how it is developed, and when it ends. A couple of well-known thematic examples occur in the fourth movement of Mozart's Symphony no. 40 in G minor (K. 550). Another great example is the fourth movement of Mozart's Symphony no. 39 (K. 543). Both of these examples are easily found on the Internet.

For additional assignments, handouts, web links, and more, please visit the web resource at www.HumanKinetics.com/MusicFundamentalsForDance.

Texture

*The word [*texture* as used in music] is adopted from textiles, where it refers to the weave of the various threads—loose or tight, even or mixed. A cloth such as tweed, for instance, leaves the different threads clearly visible. In fine silk, the weave is so tight and smooth that the individual constituent threads are hard to detect.*

Joseph Kerman,
American music critic and musicologist (b. 1924)

To understand musical texture, you need to understand what the term *texture* means when applied to both music and dance. In music, texture describes the layering of sounds in a composition. Texture in music is classified as monophonic, homophonic, or polyphonic. There may be only one melody (monophonic texture); there may be several (contrapuntal or polyphonic textures). Texture may also refer to the number of instruments playing and what parts they are playing in relationship to each other. It may describe the harmonies that support a melody, homophonic texture (melody with accompaniment), or several melodies.

Texture in dance is very similar to texture in music; obviously, instead of being auditory, it is visual. For dancers, teachers, and choreographers, understanding musical texture helps in their analysis of music and in their ability to select music for choreography, composition studies, and class exercises. In dance, the ability to correlate the texture of a music composition to the number of dancers performing is very desirable. It can be unsettling to see one dancer performing to a booming symphonic score where the volume of the music and the number of instruments might overpower a single dancer. It may also be awkward to see a large number of dancers performing to a solo instrument. The volume, dynamics, and timbre of one instrument or voice may not be enough to support the movement of many dancers; the music might sound comparatively weak. There are also instances where these examples do work— one instrument and several dancers or many instruments and one dancer. But the point of this chapter is musical texture, the interweaving of voices (vocal or instrumental) to create depth, power, harmony, and musical effects—to create music. To help you understand the importance of these concepts, this chapter discusses the various types of musical texture, contrapuntal devices, and nonimitative polyphony.

Three Types of Musical Texture

In music, texture occurs simultaneously with the melody. The three kinds of musical texture are monophony, homophony, and polyphony. That is, a melody can be heard alone, harmonized, or played simultaneously with others.

Texture in dance lends dimension and complexity to movement. It relates to the audience members' perception of how dancers look individually or in a group and how they are moving. It can also describe the difficulty of the movement as well as how the dancers perceive the movement through their own bodies. Dance texture describes either the number of dancers moving or the number and type of movements performed simultaneously. There may be one dancer moving alone, many dancers moving in unison, many dancers moving many different ways, or one dancer moving in contrast to others. Returning to musical texture, the most basic classification as well as the most ancient is monophony.

Monophony

Monophony is music composed of only a single melodic line, such as a melody made up of one voice and no accompanying instruments. The music composed before the advent of music notation is monophonic. Before the 10th century C.E., all music was monophonic. Even today, countries such as China, Japan, India, Java, Bali, Saudi Arabia, Iran, Iraq, Turkey, and Egypt provide examples of their cultures' monophonic music as a predominant musical texture. Traditional Native American songs and chants are also examples of monophonic music.

One or several voices or instruments may play monophonic music. If there are several instruments playing in unison, they must be playing the same melody in order to qualify as monophonic texture.

Many countries continue to use monophonic music in their cultures, which can provide an interesting accompaniment for solo dance work.

Artist: Smt. Jaya Mani; Photographer: R. Venkatesh

The instruments may play the melody in different octaves. This still qualifies the unison voices or instruments as monophonic. If several instruments are playing something other than the melody (if they are playing harmonies or other melodies), the music is not considered monophonic. Examples of monophonic music are unison and unaccompanied singing of "Mary Had a Little Lamb" and "London Bridge." Also do a web search for a Gregorian chant, which is a great illustration of monophonic texture. In figure 4.1 notice how the sopranos start out in unison, divide into three parts (marked *div.*), and then return to a unison line (marked *unis.*) thus starting and ending in monophony.

Note that percussion instruments playing along with a melody do not affect the qualification of monophony. Monophony refers to the tonal texture of music (the melody), not the rhythmic texture of the music. The music's rhythm is embellishment of the melody, not a part of it.

The term *monophonic* is not used in dance. Dancers speak of solo works, solo dancers, or a group of dancers moving in unison.

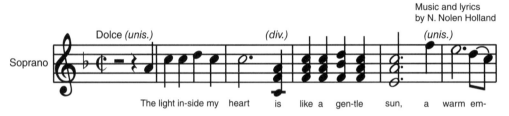

Figure 4.1 Sopranos singing in unison, then in three parts, and then in unison again.

Homophony

Homophony is a musical texture based on a melody and its accompanying harmonies. The harmonies are provided through chords: two or more pitches sounding at the same time, one of which will be the melodic pitch. Chords harmonize with, include, and enhance the melody. The sacred choral traditions (religious choral music) of the Middle Ages and the Renaissance, spawned homophonic texture in the baroque era. Many religious hymns date back over 500 years. Hymns are just one example of homophonic texture. Homophonic music was the preferred musical texture between 1750 and 1900.

In the hymn "Amazing Grace," the soprano part of the hymn is the melody. The alto, tenor, and bass parts supply harmony in which there is rarely any rhythmic variation. This means that the alto, tenor, and bass parts are pitches that relate to and harmonically embellish the soprano part's pitches. Generally, in hymns the soprano part is the melody. In hymnal and folk homophonic music, the vocal parts generally move in the same rhythmic pattern. In fact, the music would become another texture were the parts to become independent of the soprano melody and do anything other than provide harmony.

Most of us have listened to music with homophonic texture since childhood. Pop music, blues, and folk music are just a few examples of music with a homophonic texture; they are generally a melody supported and embellished by chords. A great deal of homophonic music developed during the period of 1750 to 1900.

In dance, a concept comparable to music's homophony is a soloist performing similarly but in slight contrast to a group. The visual focus is on the soloist, but the group's movement supports, embellishes, or enhances the soloist's movement. Maybe a soloist and a group dance the same movements, but the soloist performs the movements more slowly so that the soloist's action looks different from the group's action because of the timing of the movements.

Polyphony

Polyphony consists of at least two independent melodies. These independent melodies are approximately equal in importance in a piece of music. The resulting harmonies and varied rhythms might add interest to the two melodies. Therefore, the major difference between homophony and polyphony is that homophony has one melody and polyphony has two or more melodies occurring simultaneously. Drumming is not usually considered melodic. Texture in drumming could be referred to as polyphonic if drums of different pitches play, such as timpani, and if the drum composition is intended to be melodic. Texture in music implies that the music is composed for an instrument capable of melodic pitches. As stated previously, a monophonic melody may be accompanied by drumming although an entire percussion section playing together would certainly create a more dense texture than a woodblock and triangle playing together.

What makes polyphony so unique among cultures? Polyphonic music began in the Middle Ages as the compositional form for sacred choral music in Europe's great cathedrals. By the baroque era, its use had transitioned into European instrumental music where it became highly developed. In concert music, the use of polyphony continues to the present day. Some music scholars argue that polyphony existed in world music forms before its use in Europe.

For examples of polyphonic music, listen to works by J.S. Bach, such as his Toccata and Fugue in D Minor, BWV 565, or one of his two-part inventions for piano. Or listen to a four-part chorus selection from Handel's oratorio *The Messiah*. See if your school has a music database that contains "For Unto Us a Child Is Born." You can also find this choral selection on the web. In the example in figure 4.2, can you see in the first measure where the opening melodic motive is stated first with the right hand and then repeated in the left? In the second measure, Bach moves the motive up a fifth and slightly alters it; then, the left hand repeats the motive beginning on the same pitch, a G, an octave lower.

TRACK 36: "For Unto Us a Child Is Born" from Handel's *Messiah*. This song exemplifies polyphony.

Polyphonic music reached a height of popularity in the 15th and 16th centuries. From 1600 to 1750, polyphonic and homophonic music coexisted. As mentioned previously, homophonic music was the preferred compositional texture between 1750 and 1900. Drawing from the musical style and techniques of the Middle Ages and the Renaissance, 20th-century composers also employed polyphony in their works.

Figure 4.2 First staff of Bach's Two-Part Invention no. 1.
Reprinted from J.S. Bach, 1927, *Two part invention no. 1* (New York: G. Schirmer, Inc.), 2.

Inherent in polyphonic music is the use of contrapuntal devices. In many instances, this concept is applicable to dance composition, although dance does not use the term *polyphony*.

Counterpoint

Music scholars define the Latin roots of the term **counterpoint** as *punctus contra punctus* (point against point) or *punctus contra punctum* (point against point), or *punctum contra punctum* (note against note). As a result, scholars use the terms *polyphony* and *counterpoint* interchangeably. Though the technique of counterpoint developed in the Middle Ages and evolved into several applications, musicians now use the term in varied ways: to describe the technique of writing polyphonic music, to refer to one voice of a multiple voice texture, or as a synonym for polyphony. Setting polyphony and counterpoint within a time frame can clarify the terms. The term *polyphony* applies to early music, and the term *counterpoint* applies to music from the later periods (17th to 18th centuries). Therefore, when discussing polyphony and counterpoint, be clear about your intended meaning.

Usually, student composers are required to study, learn, and compose music employing contrapuntal devices. As a dancer, you should also be familiar with the following tools of music composition because the concepts apply to both dance and music composition. The more familiar choreographers are with these techniques or devices, the more insight they can develop about the interrelationship of dance and music and that relationship to their compositions. As a result, choreographers' work might also demonstrate more creativity and clarity. Choreographers who are familiar with these compositional techniques are also able to make sophisticated decisions regarding the relationship of their choreography to the music, such as creating movement that is a visual counterpoint to the music or creating movement that is different from the phrasing and structure of the music.

Imitative Contrapuntal Devices

When each voice (vocal or instrumental) uses the same melodic material as it enters the musical fabric, it is termed **imitation** or **imitative counterpoint**. The restating of the melody in different voices may be exact or merely suggestive of the melody. When it is exact, it is also called **imitative counterpoint**. The following discussion defines six melodic manipulation techniques.

Canon

A **canon** is the strictest form of musical imitation. It starts when a melody begins; it may be vocal or instrumental. At a predetermined place in the first melody, a second voice or instrument begins and states the same melody exactly as the first voice. This is referred to as imitative counterpoint as mentioned previously. The time

> **TRACK 37:** Music with canon counterpoint: the French folk tune, "Frère Jacques."

interval between when the first voice begins its melodic statement and when the second voice joins in with its own melodic statement creates harmonic and rhythmic counterpoint. Two to five voices make up most canons. In a canon, the imitation must be exact and continue throughout the work.

The two types of canons are **finite** and **infinite** (or **perpetual**). Composers predetermine the length of the finite canon. Some of Bach's *Two-Part Inventions* are examples of the finite canon. Johann Pachelbel's Canon in D is one of the most famous canons from the classical music tradition. You are probably most familiar with the infinite canon because you learned several examples as a child. These infinite canons, such as "Three Blind Mice," "Row, Row, Row Your Boat," "Frère Jacques," and "White Choral Bells," can repeat endlessly. Infinite canons are commonly known as rounds. Usually, a round is repeated as many times as there are people or groups singing the round. The distance in time for a round is a complete phrase and the distance of the interval is unison (usually implying an octave if men and women are singing together). This means that

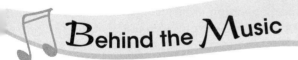

Behind the Music

Nonimitative Counterpoint

There is also a type of nonimitative counterpoint where the second and third voices do not exactly restate the first voice melody but do complement the first voice harmonically. Nonimitative counterpoint is similar to a canon in that each voice enters at a prescribed time interval, though sometimes both voices enter simultaneously.

one person or one group sings the first phrase of the canon, such as "Row, Row, Row Your Boat." As the first person or group begins the next phrase, "gently down the stream," the second person or group begins singing, "row, row, row your boat," which overlaps with the first person or group's singing of "gently down the stream." When the first group starts singing, "merrily, merrily, merrily, merrily," a third person or group could begin with "row, row, row your boat." Each person or group can continue to sing the canon until each group has sung the complete song the desired number of times (see figure 4.3).

In dance, the technique of the canon is a choreographic device as well as a dance structure. The canon is often a common dance composition assignment in which students create a movement phrase and then overlap and develop the phrase. The canon, as a structure, has been the basis for many dance works.

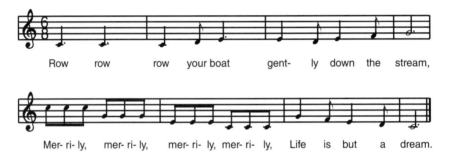

Figure 4.3 The music and lyrics for "Row, Row, Row Your Boat."
Reprinted from 8notes.com

Inversion

Musical inversion is relatively simple in concept, yet it follows a prescribed mathematical formula. **Inversion** means turning the melodic contour in the opposite direction from its original statement. Where a melody moved upward, through inversion, it changes to move downward. In other words, this imitation is a type of musical mirroring based on the first note or interval of the phrase. This technique is also called **contrary motion** and, if the inversions overlap, becomes the imitation technique of **canon inversion**. Many of Bach's dances display melodic inversion, specifically the allemandes from both Bach's Partita in G major and the *French Suite in B minor*. There is an example of inversion in Bach's *Quarendo invenietis* canon from his *Musical Offering*, BWV 1079. You can see and hear this at www.teoria.com/reference/i/inversion_counter. php?I=F. Figure 4.4 shows an original melody and then the inverted version of the melody.

In dance, with just a body, true inversion is virtually impossible. However, in aerial dance, every sort of inversion is possible. An alternative, mirroring, is a common technique in dance composition. In inversion dependent on a dancer's body alone, the dancer's upper body and arm strength or acrobatic ability is the only limit. Dancers can also suspend from cables or fabric, as in aerial dance, or have other dancers support them. It is a given that in dance, inversion limits or eliminates the mobility of the dancers' arms or legs. Inver-

Figure 4.4 An original melody with the inverted version of the same melody.

sion in dance, if done without cables, fabric, or another person, is difficult to sustain. If inversion is performed suspended in the air by fabric or cables, a dancer's mobility and ability to invert are more fully optimized.

Retrograde

The **retrograde** form of melodic manipulation is playing the pitches backward beginning with the last note and moving backward through the melody to the first note. Look at figure 4.5. Do you see how the last note becomes the first in the retrograde? Although it is an example of a retrograde canon, listen to and watch Michael Monroe's animations of Bach's *Musical Offering* on the Internet.

In dance composition, retrograde requires great skill of the choreographer and dancer. The dancer must start with the last movement performed and move through the phrase in order from last to first. In both dance and music, the technique of retrograde motion will probably go unnoticed by the audience. Retrograde as a compositional technique will be more appreciated by the choreographer or composer and the performers.

Figure 4.5 Original melody and retrograde of the melody.

Retrograde Inversion

From reading the descriptions, you can quickly surmise the outcome of combining the two melodic devices of retrograde and inversion. A **retrograde inversion** is a musical structure and melodic technique that is performed from last note to first with the melody inverted; the lower tones would be played in their higher-pitch equivalent and the higher notes would be played in their lower-pitch equivalent beginning with the last note and moving backward through the composition to the first note (see figure 4.6).

Figure 4.6 A melody and its retrograde inversion.

In dance, retrograde inversion would be possible with much practice. Retrograde inversion moves from the last movement to the first movement while at the same time mirroring or changing the body's position, inverting it. If a dancer cannot turn his body upside down, for example, perhaps moving to the other side, in an opposite direction, performing an aerial version of it, or performing the movement phrase in another plane would also work.

Augmentation and Diminution

The last two contrapuntal devices, augmentation and diminution, relate to musical time. **Augmentation** means lengthening the original time value of the melody's notes. The augmentation process is calculated mathematically. Sometimes in music, augmentation occurs in an accompanying voice right along with the statement of the melody. **Diminution** is the opposite of augmentation, because the note values are shortened. In the contrapuntal device of diminution, a last imitative technique, the melody has decreased time values. Therefore, the time it takes to play the melody diminishes. The composer or arranger determines the decrease in time. In diminution (and augmentation), a composer or arranger might change the time signature as well. Look at the examples of augmentation and diminution from Bach's *Well-Tempered Clavier Book II* in figures 4.7 and 4.8. Look at the first measure of Fugue no. 2 in C Minor. That melodic material becomes augmented in the tenor voice (the top set of notes on the bass staff) in measures 14 and 15 (see figure 4.7). In Fugue no. 9 in E Major, the melodic material from the first two measures receives a diminution treatment in the tenor voice beginning on the second note of measure 28 (see figure 4.8).

In dance composition, it may or may not be as easy to slow a dancer's movements. For example, if a dancer is moving to music or percussion sounds, it is relatively simple to double the time length of a dancer's movements based on the meter. However, if a dance is not performed to music, a dancer's performance might be less precise when she is asked to slow the movement. The dancer's skill and the choreographer's coaching will determine the success of using augmentation as an imitative device.

In the case of choreographic diminution, dancers perform movements faster, sometimes by being asked to perform movement in one count where previously they had been assigned two counts to each movement. Besides the obvious reason of giving choreographers and composers a way to speed up movement and melodies, diminution enables development or expansion of movement phrases and melodies, respectively.

Figure 4.7 *(a)* Measure 1 from Bach's Fugue no. 2 in C Minor and *(b)* its augmentation from measures 14 and 15.

(a) Reprinted from J.S. Bach, 1740, Fugue no. 2 in C minor. In *The well-tempered clavier,* book 2 (Boca Raton, FL: The Well-Tempered Press, Masters Music Publications, Inc.), 11. *(b)* Reprinted from J.S. Bach, 1740, Fugue no. 2 in C minor. In *The well-tempered clavier,* book 2 (Boca Raton, FL: The Well-Tempered Press, Masters Music Publications, Inc.), 11.

Figure 4.8 *(a)* Measures 1 and 2 from Bach's Fugue no. 9 in E Major and *(b)* the diminution in measures 28 and 29 in both the tenor and bass voices.

(a) Reprinted from J.S. Bach, 1740, Fugue no. 2 in C minor. In *The well-tempered clavier,* book 2 (Boca Raton, FL: The Well-Tempered Press, Masters Music Publications, Inc.), 42. *(b)* Reprinted from J.S. Bach, 1740, Fugue no. 2 in C minor. In *The well-tempered clavier,* book 2 (Boca Raton, FL: The Well-Tempered Press, Masters Music Publications, Inc.), 42, 43.

Nonimitative Polyphony

TRACK 38:
Music with non-imitative polyphony. Individual pieces are played separately and then together for nonimitative polyphony.

When different melodies occur at the same time, the polyphony is nonimitative. For instance, when jazz musicians improvise together, they play in the same key, and they improvise within the same meter. Yet, their individual improvisations may sound like independent melodies. The musicians may be playing in the same key and meter, yet their melodies may or may not be related. If the melodies are not related, then what they are doing is called **nonimitative polyphony**. The song "Pick a Little, Talk a Little" from *The Music Man* is an example of nonimitative polyphony. Although the melodies of the two songs "Pick a Little, Talk a Little" and "Good Night Ladies" are performed in the same key, they are two standalone melodies that are heard at the same time.

Applying the principle of nonimitative polyphony to dance would be simple. Within a dance, there could be two solos occurring at the same time. The two soloists dance to the same music. But their movements do not relate to each other, share the same movements, or look similar to each other.

Two dancers demonstrating the concept of nonimitative polyphony through two different movement styles, lyrical and tap.

Polyphonic Simultaneity

Nonimitative polyphony is different from **polyphonic simultaneity**. Polyphonic simultaneity occurs when two melodies are heard at the same time. However, in polyphonic simultaneity, melodies may not be in the same key. They may not share the same time signature or have any other musical elements in common. The music of American composer Charles Ives (1874-1954) has many examples of simultaneity. Ives created music that was perhaps ahead of its time. His third symphony received a Pulitzer Prize in 1947. Within the same piece of music, Ives would juxtapose simultaneous melodies played by what sounded like an orchestra and a marching band. An example is to think of what it would sound like if a student were listening to rock or rap music and someone walked into the room singing an operatic aria. This would constitute musical simultaneity for the length of time that the two musical styles coexisted.

TRACK 39: Music with polyphonic simultaneity. Individual pieces are played separately and then together for polyphonic simultaneity.

In dance, choreographer Merce Cunningham employed perhaps the most similar dance compositional structure to music's polyphonic simultaneity. He often had dancers performing simultaneously in various areas of the stage. His work often challenged the audience to choose where to focus their attention. An example of Cunningham's use of simultaneous focus, his dance compositional technique similar to polyphonic simultaneity, occurred in his 1999 work *Biped*. Cunningham presented computer-generated holographic images and dance images simultaneously with movement of live dancers. In another example, two totally different dances occurring simultaneously, such as a *Swan Lake* pas de deux danced to its music and a tap dance to the music of *42nd Street*, is a dance simulation of the music principle of polyphonic simultaneity.

Summary

After reading about melody, rhythm, and types of texture, you should investigate how these elements combine in Western music. Regarding texture, one mark of excellent dancers is their understanding of the relationship between their own movement and the movement of other dancers in a choreographer's work without having to be told to watch the other dancers. An excellent dance composition teacher might guide you through various exercises that develop your understanding of and ability to create dance studies with various kinds of texture. Excellent choreographers might intrigue, astound, and draw in their audiences with their works' infinite varieties of textures. Completing the practical applications at the end of the chapter will allow you to internalize your knowledge of texture and gain initial experiences with music textures.

Practical Applications

Supplementary Exercises, Activities, and Projects

1. Monophonic music: In class or individually, listen to music from cultures where the predominant musical texture is monophonic. Hint: Be sure to listen for whether several instruments (or voices) are playing the melody in unison as opposed to a few playing a melody and the rest providing harmony. Remember that texture in music implies that the music is composed for an instrument capable of melodic pitches and that a monophonic melody may be accompanied by drumming.

2. Imitative techniques project in contrapuntal devices: As a class, sing one of the infinite canons listed in the chapter. Is this an easy task for dancers? Next, in the classroom or dance studio, replicate a dance version of the infinite canon that you just sang. This may be done with small groups. Perform the completed works for the class. This dance project may also be applied to the other contrapuntal devices of inversion, retrograde, retrograde inversion, augmentation, and diminution. Different groups may be assigned different imitative techniques on which to base their group composition. A follow-up exercise is to combine or juxtapose the group dances.

3. Nonimitative polyphony: Listen to Charles Ives' music (e.g., "The Circus Band" or the fifth movement of his Second Symphony, Allegro Molto Vivace). Then, as a class, create your own nonimitative polyphonies by playing or singing two or more different melodies simultaneously.

For additional assignments, handouts, web links, and more, please visit the web resource at www.HumanKinetics.com/MusicFundamentalsForDance.

Reading Music Scores

Y
ou must have the score in your head, not your head in the score.

Hans von Bülow,
German conductor, pianist, arranger, and composer
(1830-1894)

A conductor and musicians use a music score for practice as well as for performance. At a concert, musicians often read the music as they play. Even though they have probably spent hours practicing the music before the performance, as musicians play through the music, they follow the music and turn the pages. Solo musicians and singers often memorize the music that they will perform. In fact, conductors, even though the score may be on the music stand in front of them, probably have rehearsed and performed the music so much that they may only need to glance at the score while conducting.

This chapter discusses the specific points that define a music score, introduces a variety of music scores and a brief history of each, and examines the usefulness of a music score to dancers, choreographers, and teachers.

A score in music is comparable to a play's script or a dance work's notation. A play's script includes all of the parts for every actor. A dance notation score includes all of the movements for every dancer. In the case of a **music score**, the part of every voice or instrument is listed with all of the composer's directions on how the parts should be performed. Whether the score is for a single instrument or for 20, as long as it includes every part for instruments or voices, it is a score. The term *score* comes from the vernacular for writing music. In a score, which is the compilation of the parts of a music work, all of the parts are vertically aligned, showing what each voice and instrument is doing at any

Music scores provide a map of what every instrument and voice should do to create a cohesive performance.

This file is licensed under the Creative Commons Attribution-Share Alike 3.0 Unported. Dublin Philharmonic Orchestra in performance, Tchaikovsky 4th Symphony, by Derek Gleeson.

point in the work. If it is a music score for a dance work, the composer may even note specific dance cues.

A composer completes a music score before musicians can play or perform it. What does dance have to do with a music score? Why should dancers study the precepts of musical scores? Imagine a composer handing a score of the music he has written for a choreographer's dance to the dancer along with an audio recording of the work. What would the dancer do with the music score? What can it reveal about the music? How can it inform the dancer and the choreography?

Value of Reading Scores

Today, if a composer and a choreographer were collaborating, the composer would probably give the choreographer a compact disc or send the choreographer a digital file electronically. Very few would give the choreographer a score unless he asked for one. Many choreographers work solely from audio recordings as they create movement. With the advent of composition programs on personal computers, a composer can create a recording of the synthesized score as well as print the score if needed.

Digital audio recordings are easy to share. Composers may send recordings to a choreographer for whom they are creating a work so the choreographer can select music he desires or approve of a composition. Dance musicians may market their recordings to dance teachers and choreographers via the Internet. Musicians and composers may post their works on Internet sites to make them available to dancers, choreographers, and teachers. Conversely, choreographers may search the Internet or their local libraries' digital files or sound recordings for music that will inspire movement for a dance work. On the Internet, they may look specifically for a musician to perform live music or for a composer with whom to collaborate. So, returning to the hypothetical instance of a choreographer referring to a printed score in today's digital age, why would a choreographer want to look at a hard copy of a score? There are a variety of reasons.

Musicians need to be able to practice their parts individually before coming together to practice the work as a group. Conductors need a full score in order to know what each solo instrument or voice is supposed to play or sing and when each group of musicians, who are playing the same type of instruments, begins and ends their phrases and sections. In the case of reconstructed or restaged dance works, a choreographer can refer to the music score to see if the composer made notations for the choreographer regarding specific parts or specific places in the music, the work's scenes, or the actual dance movement. If possible, when reconstructing or rechoreographing an existing work, a choreographer should consult the score before beginning to choreograph, whether the work is a Broadway musical revival, a new ballet, or the dances in a play or opera. The score is useful even if the choreographer is using a recording of the music to develop movement. The score provides the choreographer with a variety of insights about the music of the play, musical, ballet, or opera.

In a music score, the sections of the work, their sequence, the length of each section based on the number of measures, the composer's prescribed tempos, the meters, the instrumentations, and the dynamic markings are visible. This information provides a starting point for choreographers. Without listening to a recording, a choreographer can ascertain the tempo of sections, the timbre of the music (which instruments are playing and thus the general tone quality of the music based on the instrumentation), and the overall texture based on the number of instruments the composer has listed in the score. In the practical applications at the end of the chapter are suggestions for analyzing simple scores. These exercises provide beginning points for first-time score readers.

It is important to know that scores vary in complexity. Following are four suggestions for beginners who are trying to read a score while listening to a recording of the music (Fiske 1959):

1. Look at the tempo mark before the music begins. (This refers to the words which describe the tempo or numbers written above the top staff, which indicate the composer's suggestion for the number of beats per minute.)

2. Follow the first violin part. Secondarily, if the melody is not apparent in the violins, look at the woodwinds or brass lines to locate the melody.

3. Look for characteristic rhythmic groups and repeated melodic phrases.

4. Look at what the other instruments are playing.

Perhaps the score for a solo voice or instrument is the most simple to read and understand.

Solo Instrument or Vocal Score

As discussed in chapter 1, the music for one voice or a solo instrument is on a single staff (see figure 1.6). If the voice or instrument has piano accompaniment, the staff for the solo voice or instrument is scored above the grand staff. The staffs of the voice or solo instrument and the bar lines of the piano staffs align with each other so that the singer or instrumentalist and the pianist can begin together and remain together, measure by measure, while they are performing the music (see figure 5.1). If the instrumentalist or vocalist has an orchestral accompaniment (as in an opera, oratorio, or a classical concerto), the solo part is scored just above the string parts (see figure 5.2). To the beginning score reader, the solo violin (violino principale) part appears to be in the middle of the score. In this example, the concerto orchestration is for a **chamber orchestra** (two oboes, two French horns, and the usual complement of string instruments plus the solo violin). A chamber orchestra uses many of the instruments of the orchestra but in smaller numbers, often omitting some of a full orchestra's groups. For a **full orchestra**, the music score could include piccolos, flutes, clarinets, oboes, bassoons, percussion instruments, trumpets, trombones, French horns, and tubas plus strings.

TRACK 40: The first movement from Mozart's Violin Concerto no. 1 in B-Flat Major, K. 207.

Cantique de Noël

Christmas Song

Edited by Carl Deis

Adolphe Adam

Figure 5.1 Example of a vocal score with piano accompaniment: the first three measures of *Cantique de Noël*. Music by Adolphe Adam, arranged by Carl Deis.

CAN TIQUE DE NOEL

Music by Adolphe Adam

Arranged by Carl Deis

Figure 5.2 Example of a solo instrument in a chamber orchestra score: the opening six measures of Mozart's Violin Concerto no. 1 in B-Flat Major, K. 207.

Reprinted from W.A. Mozart, 1775, *Violin concerto no. 1 in B-flat major, K. 207* (New York: Edwin F. Kalmus).

Piano Score

As discussed in chapter 1, a **piano score** is a series of grand staffs (see figure 5.3). This particular example by Hans Liné is of interest to dancers because it is music inspired by the **two-step** dance form. Try clapping the rhythm of the treble (the right hand staff). Does the rhythm lend itself to movement? Is it lively? After you study this relatively simple example of a score, the next logical step is to discuss scores for more than one instrument.

Figure 5.3 A piano score: a page from Hans Liné's "Belle of Richmond" (1902).
Reprinted from Jos. W. Stern & Co. Copyright MCMII.

Scores for Two or More Instruments or Voices

When music is for two or more instruments or voices, usually each instrument or voice's part is on its own staff. The music for a string quartet looks like the example in figure 5.4. As the illustration shows, the **string quartet score** has four staffs, one for each instrument of the quartet. Note the use of the C clef (or alto clef) for the viola and the use of the F clef (bass clef) for the cello.

TRACK 41: The first movement from Mozart's Quartet no. 13 in D Minor, K. 173.

As the number of instruments increases, so does the number of staffs on the score. Depending on whether the score is for a quintet, octet, or chamber orchestra, the number of staffs will match the number or type of instruments the composer has selected. Scores for choruses with piano accompaniment have a similar yet different sort of score.

Music for a **chorus** accompanied by a piano may have three to six staffs, one staff for each voice or each specified vocal group (e.g., sopranos, mezzo sopranos, and altos which make up a women's chorus) and usually two staffs (a grand staff) for the piano accompaniment. A chorus is a vocal group that may be composed of all men or boys, all women or girls, or both men and women or boys and girls. The composition of a women's chorus is soprano I, soprano II, and alto or soprano I, soprano II, alto I, and alto II. A men's chorus is composed of tenor, baritone, and bass voices. It is also possible that two or more vocal parts appear on one staff with the divided parts appearing similar to **chords**.

It is possible that a choreographer may be asked to create a dance to be performed while a chorus is singing. If no recording of the music is available, the choreographer could refer to the chorus's music (see figure 5.5 for an example). Imagine trying to create a dance while the chorus was rehearsing. It would be virtually impossible. But by referring to the score, the choreographer could have an idea of the tempo, meter, and places in the music that are loud or soft. The choreographer might also be able to estimate the length of the piece. At the beginning of some scores of longer works is the total performance

Figure 5.4 An example of a string quartet score of Mozart's Quartet no. 13 in D Minor, K. 173.

Reprinted from W.A. Mozart, 1773, Quartet no. 13 in D minor, K. 173. In *Wolfgang Amadeus Mozart complete string quartets* (New York: Dover Publications, Inc.).

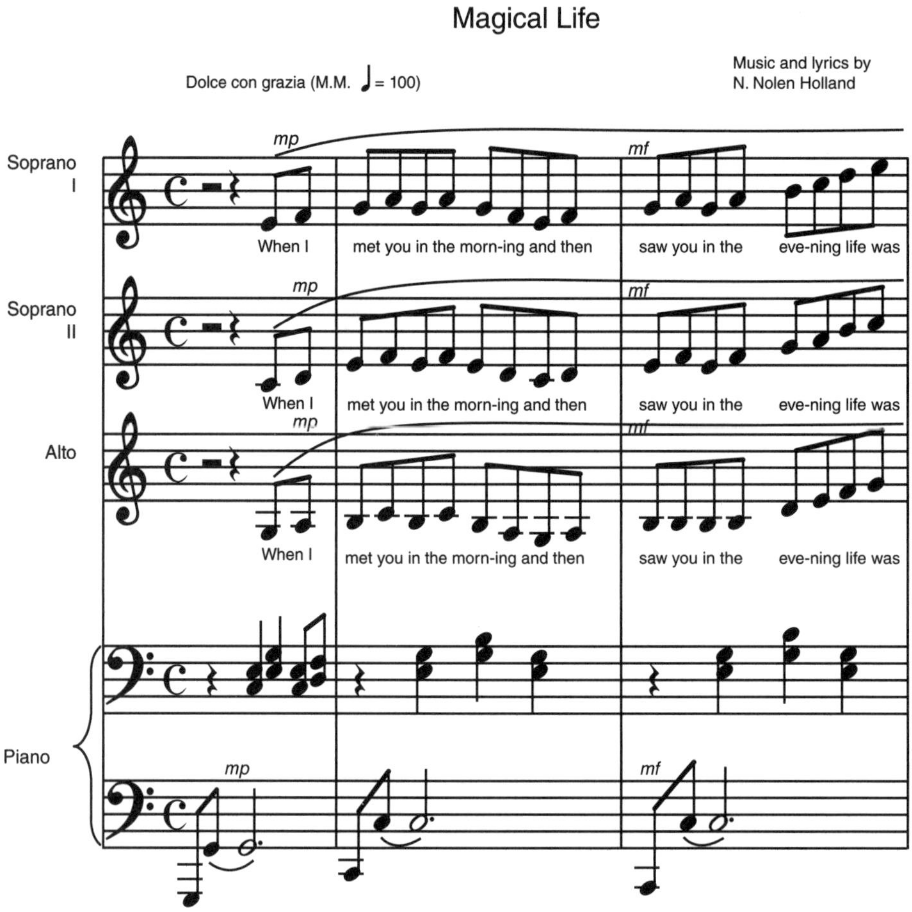

Figure 5.5 Example of a women's chorus with piano accompaniment.

time for the work along with the instrumentation and variety and number of instruments the score requires.

If a music work includes even more instruments, as in a concerto grosso or a symphony, the conductor's score, or the **full score,** includes each instrument's part. A full score shows every vocal or instrumental part separately on the same page.

In a full score, the listing of orchestral families begins at the top of the page with the woodwind instruments. Below the woodwinds are the brass instruments, then voices (if the work is a cantata, oratorio, or opera), followed by the percussion instruments and finally the strings. Each orchestral family lists instruments in order of pitch from the highest to the lowest with the exception of the horns, which appear on the brass instruments' first line because of their usual interaction with the woodwinds. Heavy brackets delineate each family (see figure 5.6). Haydn and Mozart, building on the work of their predecessors Stamitz and Gossec, standardized the instruments included in an orchestra as well as the listing of orchestral families on a score.

In a long work, a **rehearsal letter,** also known as a rehearsal mark or figure, may be above the staffs. These letters or actual bar numbers may appear intermittently throughout a work and give the conductor and musicians reference points where

Figure 5.6 Example of an orchestral score: the first 10 measures of *Acrobats of God*, by Carlos Surinach.

they can resume playing together in rehearsal. Also in a long work, rehearsal letters may signify distinct sections of the composition. The conductor may refer the orchestra or band musicians to these section demarcations so that everyone can begin in the same place in the music. Although it is only 10 measures long, look at the example of an orchestral score in figure 5.6. What do these 10 measures reveal about the beginning of the opening scene of this modern dance work created for Martha Graham? Note that each instrument's 10 measures align with all the others all the way down the page. Is it easy to read each instrument's part simultaneously while counting, "One-two, one-two, one-two, one-two"?

Other Types of Scores

Jazz and pop musicians might refer to song notation that can be quickly read and played on the spot. This kind of score comes in the form of a **fake book**. Even if they don't know a tune or melody, musicians can quickly glance at the melody and the chords to "fake" a performance of the song or tune. A fake book provides the melody on a staff with chords above the corresponding notes (see figure 5.7). Capital letters indicate chords (e.g., A, G, F). Fake books are notorious for having incorrect information and for being unauthorized. Today's published versions, which do adhere to copyright law, are readily available.

Sometimes published pop, jazz, folk, bluegrass, or blues music will have **guitar tablature** listed above the melody instead of or in addition to chords. Guitar tablature shows a musician how to play a chord with an illustration of which finger goes on which guitar fret (see figure 5.8). A **fret** is the small metal bar that divides a fret board into sections along the neck of the instrument and allows a musician to play different pitches by pressing specific fingers on specific strings between the frets. Even in published tablature, chords may not sound exactly like the recorded tune.

Other stringed instruments, such as ukuleles, mandolins, and banjos, have their own specific tablature. Even harmonicas, though they are wind instruments, have a specific tablature and symbols.

Summary

Although this chapter is a cursory presentation of music scores, it offers basic information on the varieties of scores.

Even with Fiske's suggestions for learning how to read scores and with the information contained in this chapter, a dancer or choreographer without previous training in music might be overwhelmed by trying to follow, or read, a score. If this is the case, it might be better to begin score reading by trying to follow the music for a solo instrument or for a piano. Ideally, a dancer, choreographer, or dance teacher should have musical training and should already be familiar with music notation before trying to read a score. Score reading is much more understandable with music training. If this is your first attempt at reading scores, begin simply and work up to more complex scores.

Figure 5.7 Excerpt from a fake book.

Figure 5.8 Song with guitar tablature.

Oh, What A Beautiful Mornin'

From OKLAHOMA!

Lyrics by Oscar Hammerstein II

Music by Richard Rodgers

Practical Applications

Supplementary Exercises, Activities, and Projects

1. Score reading: In class, look at various types of scores for piano, string quartet, and so on. Based on the information in the previous chapters and this chapter, analyze the scores in class with regard to notation, melody, time, texture, instrumentation, and other aspects of score analysis. Norton Scores facilitate score reading by highlighting the instruments playing the melody and are very helpful for beginning score reading. They contain a wide variety of examples.

2. Score reading: While the instructor plays a musical selection, follow along by reading the score as the music plays. This may take many attempts, even with the simplest of scores. Begin with familiar music such as holiday songs or popular music and progress to following unfamiliar but simple scores.

3. Score reading: With a solo or piano score to read, clap the rhythmic notation of the solo instrument or voice or the top line of notes from a piano score's treble staff. Be sure to establish the tempo before attempting to clap the notation.

For additional assignments, handouts, web links, and more, please visit the web resource at www.HumanKinetics.com/MusicFundamentalsForDance.

Form
and Structure

Before a company of dancers can create beauty on the stage, a choreographer must choose the steps and combine them into the right pattern for the mood and idea he wishes to express. Likewise, the musical composer shapes the elements of music into a form chosen for his purpose.

Daniel T. Politoske,
professor emeritus of musicology, University of Kansas (b. 1935)

To investigate musical form, understand its connection to dance, define various classical forms, and complete basic exercises on form and structure, you need to understand first what form is. A good place to begin is the same place critics and scholars begin: by looking at specific components of music. They look at how composers sequence phrases and sections, how composers introduce melodies or themes, how they manipulate melodic or thematic elements, and how they end a work. Naturally, variances in these components distinguish one work from another. A work's form and structure may also determine the work's popularity and longevity. Components such as the introduction, melody, sections of a work, and ending are also the basics of musical form. Each contributes to a work's structure. Additionally, a work's structure reveals the way in which a composer created and tied sections together.

In dance, whether a choreographer is creating a shorter or longer work, there is usually an introductory section (or opening), various sections with combinations of dancers (soloists, groups, soloists with groups, and so forth), and a

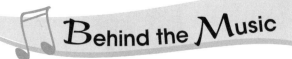

Behind the Music

Renaissance Dance and Musical Form

In the early Renaissance, dances were linked musically in pairs: a slow dance followed by a faster dance. These grouped dances led to more dances being grouped together with each one following the previous without a break. By the baroque era, composers began to separate the music from the related dances. The musical forms remained and evolved into the classical era's multimovement works. In this way, dance greatly contributed to the development of musical form.

conclusion. These are basic concepts of form and structure, whether referring to music or to dance. This final chapter includes many classical elements that composers continue to use today. Composers often give works their own personal twist by inserting their own modifications, reinventions, or creations. Especially in the discussion of musical and dance forms of past eras, you will learn of connections that dance has had to music. Documentation and notation of dance and music connections began to occur in the late Middle Ages and has continued to the present day. The writing and recording of music and dance are relatively recent in human history. How people have danced and the music to which they have danced have evolved. In music, as in dance, it is a work's structure—the way in which a composer has created and tied sections together—that distinguishes the work from others.

The standard musical genres discussed in this chapter reflect European culture from the time of the Middle Ages to the present. It is good for dancers to know that these genres are universal. Composers worldwide have written music in these forms. For a choreographer, knowing and understanding instrumental and vocal music genres may simplify a search for music. For dance teachers who use prerecorded music, mixing genres in class accompaniment expands students' classroom experiences and learning. Teachers can also relay information about the class music and genre as a transition from one exercise to the next.

Understanding Musical Form

Form is the overall organization of a piece of music. As in dance, where there are one-act ballets, evening-length story ballets, various modern dance styles, and dance theater, music has a similar variety of forms.

Musical forms have evolved out of the musical needs of a particular culture. Music has developed out of what people desired for specific occasions, what they have wanted to hear, or what musicians and composers have wanted to play and write, respectively. Some composers, especially in the 20th and 21st centuries, have created personal forms of expression rather than followed established forms. Still others have built on what has been handed down to them as a starting point for presenting their own musical ideas, but in new ways.

There is an argument among music scholars regarding the terms *form* and *structure*—which should precede and include the other. For the purposes of this chapter, form indicates the outline, the overall design of a piece of music. **Structure** refers not only to the tonal or harmonic organization of a piece of music but also to the components of the form. Therefore, form refers to the general patterns, such as binary, rondo, and sonata. Structure refers to the details of the overall design or, in other words, what constitutes the form.

With working definitions for form as the big picture of a composition and for structure as the elements of that composition, the next step is to look at basic musical forms and their structures. The best place to begin is with the simplest. Yet, composers have taken the following simple concepts and have developed them into quite complicated arrangements.

"Just as a novel, a play, or a ballet is divided into chapters or acts, scenes, episodes, and such smaller elements as paragraphs, lines, and gestures, so the progress of music in time achieves form and intelligibility through small groupings, each making its particular contribution to the development of the whole" (Wallace Berry, 1986, p. 1).

Photo courtesy of Rhyme Wan Chang.

 ## Behind the Music

David Maslanka (b. 1943): Taking Tchaikovsky's Flutter Tonguing Technique to the Next Level

For the opening of act II of *The Nutcracker*, Tchaikovsky was one of the first composers to incorporate the flute articulation technique of flutter tonguing. A little over 100 years later, in the late 20th century, composer David Maslanka had the saxophone section flutter their tongues without playing their saxophones in order to create the sound of birds in flight. He was inspired by a flock of sparrows taking off overhead when he was out walking one day. This sound was so lovely and spiritually moving that he put it into one of his largest compositions, his 1996 *Mass*. A mass is a sacred musical form for voices and instruments or voices alone.

Repetition and Contrast

Repetition and contrast are the two most basic elements of musical form. These concepts evolved as a response to the human need for comfort in the familiar and then, becoming bored with the familiar, a change to something new. Repetition and contrast also help the listener perceive musical form. The repetition of a phrase reinforces the melody and makes the listener more acquainted with it; then a new, different phrase is introduced (the contrast).

Repetition is the opposite of contrast. Repetition may be immediate (AA, meaning that a phrase may be immediately repeated without a contrast) or come after a new idea has been presented (ABA; the B section is the one contrasting the A section). In longer musical works that incorporate thematic development (e.g., sonata allegro form), when the original melodic or thematic statement (A) follows a contrasting section (B), it is restatement rather than repetition. The term *restatement* implies that the first section (the melody or theme) follows a contrasting melody or theme.

TRACK 42: Music with AA form of repetition: excerpt from "Square Dance Rock" by F. Barclay.

TRACK 43: Music with AB form of repetition and contrast.

Repetition is common to all musical forms. It may be literal, meaning exactly the same, or it may be varied. If the repetition is varied, a composer will include enough of the original statement for the listener to recognize it. In diagramming varied repetition, it is shown as A^1, meaning that the A section has repeated and is similar to A, is embellished, or is altered. Repetition, depending on the way in which the material is repeated, can also be used in creating a much longer work. Ideas may return in their original form, or they may be transformed to present nuances and therefore new meanings.

The American folk song "Polly Wolly Doodle" is a short example of repetition and contrast. In this song, the repetition comes when the second verse, or part A, returns after the chorus. The chorus presents something new to hear—a contrast from the verse. Yet, the last line of the chorus is a repeat of the last line of the verse. It brings the listener back to something familiar. Notice how the notes and the text on the third staff and the sixth staff in figure 6.1 are identical. When the phrase "Sing Polly Wolly Doodle all the day" comes at the end of the verse as well as at the end of the chorus, it is the same. This concept of repetition and contrast is found in the simple form of nursery rhymes and in more complex musical forms such as the classical concerto. This simple part A and part B formula is also a basic song form. (Note: Instrumental recordings and samples of "Polly Wolly Doodle" are readily available on the Internet if you are unfamiliar with it.)

This concept of repetition and contrast also applies to dance. Repetition in dance may be immediate and as short as a single movement. For example, the movement phrases in many of Petipa's classical-era ballet variations are often composed of three repetitions of a movement followed by a variant of the step or a different movement performed as the fourth movement in the phrase sequence. Likewise, modern dance choreographer Laura Dean built her early choreographic style on the repetitive use of spinning (turning). Knowing how to incorporate the techniques of repetition and contrast or repetition and

Figure 6.1 Verse 1 and chorus of "Polly Wolly Doodle," an example of repetition and contrast in basic song form of ABA.

restatement can greatly enhance choreographic development just as it does musical development. It can lead to expansion of a work. It gives choreographers or composers somewhere to go with their ideas, lengthening and expanding both musical works and dances.

As stated earlier, contrast is a different part of a song or musical work; it comes after a first part. In basic song form, the contrasting section may be the chorus (refrain). Generally speaking, in musical form, the contrasting section is referred to as part B simply because it follows the first section or phrase, which is usually called part A. Binary form in music means that there are distinct A and B sections in a song or work. Understanding binary (two-part) form enhances and expands this discussion of repetition and contrast.

Binary Forms

Binary form can be as simple as part A and part B, but it can also become quite complex. Simple binary form means that a work is divided into two distinct sections, AB or AA[1]. The difference between the two sections, the A section

Behind the Music

"That dance forms should enter so significantly into the history of music is not surprising in view of the inevitability and universality of the alliance of dance and music" Wallace Berry (1986, p. 322).

and the B section or the A section and A^1 section, is what establishes the form as binary. There is usually a repetition of each binary section so that a diagram of the sections would look like AABB or AAA^{1}A^1. Most binary forms begin and end clearly. The first section, the A, may end with a weaker cadence and be harmonically open. As discussed in chapter 3, when the cadence is harmonically open, it gives the listener the impression that more music will follow, that the music will continue. Sometimes the A section ends on a harmonically closed cadence and the B section has a fresh start. The second section, B, usually ends in a harmonically closed cadence, meaning that the cadence gives the listener the impression that the music has come to a harmonically closed or final conclusion. Each section is usually composed of different musical material but may share a common motive. Part B material may also be based on or drawn from part A. The two parts may be connected by a transition (link), and each may also have a codetta (a short ending section), although it is very unusual for part A to have a codetta. After parts A and B, there may be a **coda**, or a longer final section.

Baroque Binary Form

Binary form was the form of choice for many baroque composers (c.1600-1750). It was dominant in much of the era's instrumental and vocal music, especially music for dance. The popularity of the binary form continued into the 19th century.

Simple binary form is the most common form in dance movements of the early classical period, and it was still used in the later 18th and 19th centuries for short **character pieces** and for themes of theme-and-variation movements. Slow movements of concertos, the stylized dance movements of sonatas, and other multimovement works may also employ binary forms. Bach and Handel, both baroque-era composers, included many dance-based sections or movements in their suites.

Baroque Dance Suites

Among baroque-era binary forms, the suite is of special interest to dancers. A baroque dance suite consists of stylized dance music based on the actual baroque court dance forms. Many early suites have 4 movements, but in other suites there may be as many as 20 movements. Music historians credit J.S. Bach with creating a standardized suite order beginning with the **allemande**, followed by a **courant**, then a **sarabande**, and concluding with a **gigue**. These are only a few of the baroque-era court dances. The music to which each dance was performed was also given the same name. This is but one example of how music and dance of past eras were inseparable. However, it is important to remember that baroque suites consisted of stylized dances, meaning that the music has the rhythm, meter, and flavor of the actual baroque dance but was for listening, not dancing, even though it evolved from the actual music that accompanied the specific dances.

In baroque-era suites, composers often inserted other dances between the sarabande and the gigue. These dance movements might have been a **minuet, gavotte, bourrée, passepied, polonaise, rigaudon, anglaise,** or **loure.** Sometimes the suite may have had a **prelude** (an introductory musical section) or a lyric, nondance movement called an **air**, which is composed in free form or in ritornello form. **Free form** occurs when composers themselves determine the music's form; they do not follow a standard form structure. **Ritornello form** includes a short, recurring passage. Again, these stylized dance forms were binary in their musical form.

TRACK 44: Gigue movement from Suite no. 3 in D major, a Baroque dance suite by J.S. Bach.

In the 19th century, the themes for sets of variations or short character pieces used simple binary form. During the 20th century, composers revived the use of binary form in **neoclassical** music (neoclassicism was a mid-20th-century use of classicism's precepts where beauty, order, clarity, restrained emotion, and succinct statement prevail). Binary form is also a part of more complex structures and forms.

Ternary Forms

Ternary form, the most common form in music, grew out of binary form. Some scholars consider ternary form more complex than the varieties of binary forms. However, study of ternary form reveals its basic simplicity. When a song, a movement of a multimovement work, or an operatic aria has three distinct and complete sections, it qualifies as a **ternary form**. Rather than present three sections of new material, its design is actually ABA. From this pattern, you can see that the third section is the same as the first. If the first section (A) returns similar to but not exactly the same, embellished, or altered, the form is diagramed as ABA[1]. In ternary form, part A is called the statement. Part B is referred to as the departure or digression from the musical material presented in part A. The restatement of part A may be literal or varied and diagrammed as ABA (the return is literal) or ABA[1] (the return is varied). An example of ABA[1] is the da capo operatic aria of the late 17th to early 18th centuries in which the return to part A was often lavishly embellished, thus showing off the singer's ability. The term **da capo** means return to the beginning (in Italian, literally "to the head"), so when the music uses a literal return, only parts A and B of the printed music were necessary. This practice continues today. Often abbreviated D.C., wherever *da capo* appears on the music, it indicates to musicians to return to the beginning of the music. Two familiar examples of songs employing the ABA form are "Twinkle, Twinkle, Little Star" and the hymn "Joyful, Joyful, We Adore Thee," which is based on Beethoven's "Ode to Joy" from the fourth movement of his Symphony No. 9 in d minor, Op. 125 also known as the "Choral" Symphony.

Baroque Ternary Forms

Ternary design (three-part form) was very popular among composers during the baroque era. As with binary form, dance music brought about the widespread use of ternary form. Originally, at court balls, dances were grouped together in pairs termed **galanterien**. Therefore, composers grouped minuets, as well as other baroque dances, in twos. Baroque ternary form developed when musicians began to play the first minuet, the A part, twice, both before and after the second minuet, the B part. Incidentally, a baroque minuet itself may have a two- or three-part form with repeats of these various parts; when the first minuet returned, it was played without any repeats. During the baroque era, minuets existed in pairs, alternating in an ABA pattern. The second dance, the B minuet, is called the trio because in the early days it was played by three instruments.

As noted above, baroque dances were presented in pairs with the first dance and its music repeated after the second. The trio (part B) is lighter in texture and quieter. At the end of the trio is a da capo, signifying that the first section is to be played again and the dance repeated. In these baroque ternary dance forms, there is rarely a transition into the trio. Baroque ternary form also dictated that when the first minuet returned after the trio, the repetitions within the first minuet, which were played in the original statement, were omitted. In the 18th century, some composers employed the minuet and trio ternary form as the third movement of symphonic works. As a ternary vocal form, the da capo aria is the vocal counterpart of the instrumental minuet and trio. The minuet and trio form describes music that was originally created for dancing the minuet and eventually became music intended solely for listening. Use of ternary form continued into the 19th century and continues today in pop music.

19th-Century Ternary Forms

During the 19th century, romantic composers also used ternary form when writing short piano pieces known as character or salon pieces. These pieces have many titles: nocturne, prelude, romance, intermezzo, fantasia, bagatelle, and dance-derived forms such as waltz, mazurka, and polonaise. (Note: Not all character or salon pieces are written in ABA form.) Composers of the 19th century also continued to use ternary form in symphonic and operatic works. In the 20th century, composers did not abandon ternary form. Hindemith, Stravinsky, Prokofiev, Berg, and Bartok used ternary form as the basis for some of their compositions or for movements of some of their long compositions such as symphonies.

TRACK 45: Example of a waltz: Strauss' *Voices of Spring Waltz*.

Movements

A **movement** is a main section of a longer musical work. Long works such as symphonies, concertos, masses, oratorios, cantatas, suites, string quartets, and sonatas contain several movements. Symphonies usually have three or four movements though more contemporary symphonies may have more. Movements are considered closed in form, meaning that they can stand alone harmonically. They usually can be divided into sections themselves, depending on the composer's choice of the form and structure. The form usually dictates the order of the movements within a work.

Behind the Music

Waltz: Paving the Way for Today's Social Dancing

When the Viennese waltz emerged in the 19th century, it was considered scandalous because it involved a public embrace. Until the advent of the waltz, dancing couples usually danced side by side holding hands or linking arms. The waltz's popularity among Europe's young people led to its eventual acceptance. Today the waltz survives as one of the required competitive ballroom dance forms. The waltz is inseparable from its triple or compound duple meter.

Couple dancing a waltz in a closed position.

Sonata Allegro Form

Generally, the first movement of a symphony, concerto, or string quartet is in sonata allegro form, which grew out of ternary form. Some authorities prefer the term *sonata form* or *first-movement form*. But because first movements of multi-movement works are generally fast, the term *sonata allegro form* developed.

The four components of sonata allegro form are **exposition**, **development**, **recapitulation**, and **coda**. Each of these components has a specific design and purpose within the structure of the sonata allegro form. In the exposition, the composer states the themes of the movement, usually after the work's introductory opening. The exposition ends with a change in key. How the composer treats, manipulates, or expands the themes constitutes the development section. When the composer returns to (restates) the original theme, it is called the recapitulation. Just as in ternary form, the recapitulation is usually literal but may be varied. A coda is often the first movement's ending and may also be a codetta, a shorter ending. A coda or codetta is often fast paced, loud, and exciting. It was not until the era of classicism in the works of Stamitz, Haydn, and Mozart that sonata allegro form was fully developed.

Second-Movement Form

Second movements usually contrast with first movements in key and in tempo. Often there is emphasis on lyrical melody in this movement. Frequently second

Second movements in music are often slow and emphasize lyrical melody. Similarly, in dance, lyrical movement can be expressive, slow, and emotional, emphasizing the beauty of the movements.

movements are slow and employ a theme-and-variations form. The form of a second movement may also be free, sonata, rondo, or ternary. Early symphonies had just three movements, as in a **concerto**, a classical three-movement composition for a solo instrument and orchestra. Some later symphonies expanded to four movements.

Third-Movement Form

Third movements are sometimes based on the baroque minuet and trio form or on Beethoven's innovation, the scherzo and trio. *Scherzo* is Italian for joke. Beethoven, using the scherzo for the third movements of some of his symphonic works, piano sonatas, and string quartets, created light, swift, and often humorous movements in triple time. They were considered humorous because Beethoven's minuets were so fast. In general, if the third movement is a dance movement (minuet and trio), the work's fourth movement will be fast.

Fourth-Movement Form

Fourth movements are usually the finale (conclusion) of a multimovement work such as a symphony and are frequently quick in tempo. These movements may be in theme-and-variations form, sonata allegro form, fantasy form (a free form), or **rondo** form, one example of which is diagrammed ABACA. (Listen to Mozart's Rondo in A Minor, K. 511, for a short example of rondo form.) Rondo finales may be used in symphonies and string quartets. They are common in concertos and sonatas.

Today, composers may create four movements for multimovement works. Sequencing movements and designating their form evolved during the classical era (c. 1750-1825). Some Renaissance (1400-1600) and baroque (1600-1750) multimovement works may have only two movements, as in Alessandro and Domenico Scarlatti's sonatas. Multimovement works may have more than four movements, as in Beethoven's five-movement Sixth Symphony, with at least one movement written in sonata allegro form. The number and form of the movements in 20th- and 21st-century works may vary only slightly or substantially from past eras. Today, composers still order and form movements according to genre.

Variation Forms

The use of variation to expand a composition dates to the 13th century. During the 16th century, variation techniques became highly developed and were virtually inseparable from the dances of the time. The two basic types of variations that emerged were the sectional and the continuous. By the early 17th century, continuous ostinato variation forms were in wide use. In music, **ostinato** means repeated bass, melodic, or harmonic patterns. These forms were based on the 16th- and 17th-century dance forms of the **chaconne** and the **passacaglia**.

Sectional Variation

The sectional variation form is commonly known as theme and variations or variations on a theme. The sectional variation's theme is sometimes original, sometimes borrowed from folk or popular melodies, and sometimes borrowed from another composer's work.

In 1778, Wolfgang Amadeus Mozart (1756-1791) created twelve variations for piano based on the French folk song "Ah! vous dirai-je, Maman," which has the same tune as "Twinkle, Twinkle, Little Star." Because the theme has a different treatment in each variation, it constitutes a sectional variation. In the early 20th century, Hungarian composer Ernst von Dohnányi (Ernö Dohnányi, 1877-1960) used "Twinkle, Twinkle, Little Star" to create 11 variations that include etude, waltz, march, scherzo, passacaglia, and chorale variations in his *Variations on a Nursery Song for Piano and Orchestra,* op. 25 (1913). Each of these sectional variation works is available for listening online.

Continuous Variation

Continuous variations differ from sectional variations in that there are no breaks or pauses between the variations. The ending of one variation is the beginning of the next. Based on the 16th- and 17th-century Spanish dances, respectively, the chaconne and passacaglia are continuous variations done in triple meter. They employ the minor mode and are slow in tempo. The chaconne and passacaglia are musical variations written over a repeating bass line. Some music scholars claim that there is no true distinction between the chaconne and the passacaglia, and the terms are often used interchangeably. In fact, the chaconne is based on a multivoiced, harmonic theme, a succession of chords, whereas the passacaglia is a melodic, single-voiced ostinato with no harmonies in its first entry. A wonderful early example of a passacaglia is in Bach's organ Passacaglia and Fugue in C Minor, BWV 582. Early examples of the chaconne are in works by Bach (Violin Sonata no. 4, Chaconne), Handel (Ciacona in D Minor), Purcell (Chacony in G Minor for Strings), and Couperin (Chaconne). Twentieth-century composers Igor Stravinsky, who included a passacaglia in his 1953 orchestral work *Septet*, and American William Schuman in his 1941 Symphony no. 3, part I, returned to this dance form as the basis for musical variations. Philip Glass included a melodic variation passacaglia as the second movement of his 2006 Symphony no. 8.

Genres

Just as there are multiple modern dance styles and many categories of world dance, there are also many types and styles in music. Each respective type, or **genre,** of the two arts has evolved out of choreographers' or composers' need to express themselves through their art forms. In music the number of genres is quite large. Following are some of the classical genres.

Symphony, Concerto, Sonata, Quartet

Instrumental genres' titles have to do with the grouping of instruments in a particular piece of music as well as structure, form, and other traditional characteristics. For example, a **symphony** is a piece of music performed by many or all of the various orchestral instruments and usually includes instruments from the four orchestral families: woodwinds, brass, percussion, and strings. As discussed earlier, a symphony also implies that a work has at least three movements, one of which is in sonata allegro form. It may be a classical, romantic, or contemporary work. As stated earlier, a **concerto** is a type of duet between a solo instrument and an orchestra or chamber orchestra and also usually has a first movement written in sonata allegro form. A **chamber orchestra** is a smaller orchestra (up to 50 musicians). A symphony orchestra may have up to 100 musicians. In a **sonata**, a solo instrument plays alone or with piano accompaniment. The genres of **quartet**, **quintet**, and **octet** are, as they imply, a grouping of four, five, or eight instruments, respectively. The instrumental groupings are often standardized, as for a string quartet, or may be specified by the composer. Instrumentation in a string quartet is usually two violins, a viola, and a cello. A classical-era quintet typically calls for two violins, two violas, and a cello, or two violins, one viola, and two cellos.

Vocal Forms

Development of vocal forms began with the songs of a particular culture. In ancient times, further development came as priests or religious leaders invented forms to suit worship services. A Western example is the **Gregorian chant**. The early Christian church adopted and adapted ancient Jewish and Islamic chants for the Mass. During the early medieval era, Pope Gregory I (c. 540-604 C.E.) called for these chants to be notated. This moment marked the beginning of Western music notation. Cloistered monks performed these early Christian chants in a cappella style and in unison as they had been sung for centuries. **A cappella** is an Italian term translated as "in chapel style," meaning vocalists sang without accompaniment. Today the term implies that a soloist, a small number of singers, or a chorus performs with no instrumental accompaniment.

In the late Middle Ages, **motets**, songs based on Biblical texts, grew out of the Gregorian chant. Motets were also unaccompanied but had parts for two or more voices; the vocal parts were contrapuntal. At the same time, **madrigals** developed, which were secular, unaccompanied, contrapuntal songs. The late Middle Ages also witnessed a variety of solo secular vocal forms, the most famous perhaps being troubadours' poetry set to song in northern French courts, which could constitute prototypes of today's love songs. Eventually, the Renaissance gave birth to art and entertainment styles.

During the Renaissance, sacred polyphonic choral styles flourished in Europe's great cathedrals. At the same time, secular dance and music were central to court entertainments. Together, music and dance contributed to the development of opera. By the baroque era, opera had become very popular. It was the time of the da capo aria. An **opera** is a dramatic or comic stage production for a chorus and solo vocalists who sing and act out an elaborate story set to orchestral accompaniment. A chorus includes standard groupings of women's and men's voices (soprano, alto, tenor, and bass) along with vocal soloists (usually soprano, alto, tenor, and baritone or bass). Large-scale opera productions with costumes and scenery brought about construction of opera houses all over Europe. Opera's standard elements are **recitative** (words spoken on a pitch or in between sung phrases), solo arias, and chorus songs. Opera is the ancestor of today's musical comedies and reached high points of development in the late 18th century, 19th century, and early 20th century.

TRACK 52:
Example of an operatic duet with chorus: "Libiamo ne' lieti calici" ("Let's drink from the joyful cup") from Verdi's *La Traviata*.

TRACK 53:
Example from an oratorio: "Hallelujah Chorus" from Handel's *Messiah*.

Dating to the baroque era as well, **cantatas** and **oratorios** are full-length vocal works for a chorus, soloists, and orchestra. Unlike the libretti (written texts) for operas, the texts of cantatas and oratorios are biblical and are usually performed without scenery or costumes. Works from the time of Bach and Handel up to the present day include vocal solos (arias) along with recitative and chorus sections. Some of the most famous oratorios are those of George Frideric Handel, such as *The Messiah* and *Israel in Egypt*. J.S. Bach also wrote cantatas linked to the church's calendar.

In the 19th century, music's romantic era, the art song evolved as an independent work for a solo voice with piano accompaniment. That 19th-century solo song tradition eventually led to 20th-century American vocal blues forms and to popular song, which has been present in some form throughout human history.

Summary

As world cultures more closely interact during the 21st and future centuries, musical forms may remain as they are, expand, or be completely abandoned and forgotten. When global cultures interact, there is great potential for new forms and new fusions of forms to develop. Students', teachers', and choreographers' exposure to and study of world dance and music have the potential to influence theatrical dance and music forms. As current educational practices require, study of music and dance forms is essential.

This chapter has outlined some basic musical forms. Armed with this information, you will be poised to continue your own studies in music and dance guided by your personal interests and projects. This chapter and the preceding chapters are not all encompassing. They merely open the door to further music studies for students, choreographers, and teachers.

Practical Applications

Supplementary Exercises, Activities, and Projects

1. Repetition and contrast: Locate the music and lyrics to Peter Yarrow's song "Puff the Magic Dragon" or any other popular folk song. With your instructor or a fellow student leading the class, sing the song in its entirety as an exercise in repetition and contrast.

2. Binary dance suite form: Listen to suites by Bach or Handel. With each movement, listen to how the music evokes or implies a particular feeling, especially for movement. For a project, research the dance forms related to the movements of the particular suite. Report on the era of each dance. Describe the meter, speed, and rhythmic characteristics of the dance. Tell about the formations or patterns the dance follows, who danced the dance (men, women, couples), and the country in which it originated.

3. Ternary form: Listen to a baroque-era minuet and trio. As a class, see if the sections are distinct. If the class agrees on the structure, listen to a minuet and trio form that is used as the third movement of a symphony to see if the sections are as clear as they were in the minuet and trio.

4. Sonata allegro form (first-movement form): As a class, study the first movement of a four-movement work that employs sonata allegro form. Analyze its structure by listening for elements of sonata allegro form or by using an instructor-provided study guide.

5. Second-movement form: Listen to the second movement of the work from exercise 4. Determine the form and structure of the movement.

6. Third-movement form: Listen to the third movement from the same work used in exercises 4 and 5. Determine whether it is a dance form, a minuet and trio, a scherzo and trio, or some other form.

7. Fourth-movement form: Listen to the same work's fourth movement and, as a class, determine the movement's form. Is it a theme and variations, sonata allegro, fantasy, or rondo? Seek a symphonic work to analyze on your own and present your brief analysis to the class.

8. Theme and variations: In class, listen to short theme-and-variations pieces. (See the list of Chopin pieces in chapter 3.) Determine whether they are sectional or continuous variations. Discuss the variation techniques the composer used.

9. Theme and variations (chaconne and passacaglia): In class, listen to early examples of the chaconne and passacaglia and then 20th-century versions as listed in this chapter. For the earlier works, see if the class can determine whether the ostinati are harmonic or bass. For the 20th-century works, is it possible to differentiate a chaconne from a passacaglia?

10. Genres: In class or individually, listen to jazz works, popular music, symphonies, concertos, sonatas, and quartets so that you can begin to discern the differences between these genres. Then listen for the sections of a particular song, piece, or work as guided by the instructor.

For additional assignments, handouts, web links, and more, please visit the web resource at www.HumanKinetics.com/MusicFundamentalsForDance.

Appendix: Music Tracks Available on the Web Resource

Chapter 1

Track 1—Major scale.

Track 2—Natural minor scale.

Track 3—Harmonic minor scale.

Track 4—Melodic minor scale.

Track 5—Music in a major mode: "My Baby's Foxtrot" by E. Swann.

Track 6—Music in a minor mode: "Melodrama" by R. Webb.

Track 7—Drum roll on timpani with dynamics increasing from piano to forte.

Track 8—Music using staccato: "Bransles" by C.K. Palmer.

Track 9—Music using legato: "Barbara Allen" by G. Dorset.

Chapter 2

Track 10—Music in 2/4: "Song in 2/4" by J.G. Wilson.

Track 11—Waltz in 6/8: "Tristesse" by P. Cork.

Track 12—Music in 3/4: *Blue Danube Waltz*, op. 314 by J. Strauss.

Track 13—Music in 4/4: "Song in 4/4" by J.G. Wilson.

Track 14—March in cut time: "Stars and Stripes Forever" by John Philip Sousa.

Track 15—March in 6/8: "Washington Post March" by John Philip Sousa.

Track 16—Music in 5/4: "Song in 5/4" by J.G. Wilson.

Track 17—Music in mixed meter: "Mixed Meter Melody" by J.G. Wilson.

Track 18—Music with polymeter: "Polymeter" by J.G. Wilson.

Track 19—Music in 4/4 with beats subdivided: "Subdivider" by J.G. Wilson.

Track 20—Music in largo: "Pathos" by R. Webb.

Track 21—Music in adagio: "A Lonely Tear" by E. Swann.

Track 22—Music in moderato: "A Love Nest for Two" by P. Cork.

Track 23—Music in allegro: "Bank Holiday" by A.W. Ketelbey.

Track 24—Music in presto: "Mayfair Quickstep" by E. Swann.

Track 25—Music with simple syncopation: "Fascination Rag" by P. Cork.

Track 26—Music with complex syncopation: "Smooth Work" by E. Thomas.

Chapter 3

Track 27—Music with self-contained melody: "Self Contained" by J.G. Wilson.

Track 28—Debussy's *Clair de lune* has open-ended melodies.

Track 29—Music with wide melodic range: "World Without End" by C.K. Palmer.

Track 30—Music with narrow melodic range: the "Ode to Joy" theme from the fourth movement of Beethoven's Ninth Symphony.

Track 31—Music with motivic sequences: the first movement of Beethoven's Fifth Symphony.

Track 32—Music with melodic phrase: the American folk tune, "Yankee Doodle."

Track 33—Adagio from the "Grand Pas de Deux" from Tchaikovsky's *The Nutcracker*. This piece has obvious climaxes in its melodic phrases.

Chapter 4

Track 34—Monophonic music: "Monophonia" by J.G. Wilson.

Track 35—Homophonic music: "Bringing in the Sheaves" by K. Shaw and G. Minor.

Track 36—"For Unto Us a Child Is Born" from Handel's *Messiah*. This song exemplifies polyphony.

Track 37—Music with canon counterpoint: the French folk tune, "Frère Jacques."

Track 38—Music with nonimitative polyphony. Individual pieces are played separately and then together for nonimitative polyphony.

Track 39—Music with polyphonic simultaneity. Individual pieces are played separately and then together for polyphonic simultaneity.

Chapter 5

Track 40—The first movement from Mozart's Violin Concerto no. 1 in B-Flat Major, K. 207.

Track 41—The first movement from Mozart's Quartet no. 13 in D Minor, K. 173.

Chapter 6

Track 42—Music with AA form of repetition: excerpt from "Square Dance Rock" by F. Barclay.

Track 43—Music with AB form of repetition and contrast.

Track 44—Gigue movement from Suite no. 3 in D major, a Baroque dance suite by J. S. Bach.

Track 45—Example of a waltz: Strauss' *Voices of Spring Waltz*.

Track 46—Piece played by a full symphony orchestra: the overture to Mozart's opera, *The Marriage of Figaro*.

Track 47—Example of a concerto: the third movement from Mozart's Horn Concerto no. 4 in E-flat Major, rondo allegro vivace.

Track 48—Example of a sonata: the first movement from Mozart's Piano Sonata no. 16 in C Major, allegro.

Track 49—Example of a string quartet: the fourth movement from Beethoven's String Quartet no. 8 in E Minor, op. 59, no. 2.

Track 50—Example of a Gregorian chant.

Track 51—Example of a madrigal: "Charles the Rich" by D. Greig, C. Daniels, and J. Bonner.

Track 52—Example of an operatic duet with chorus: "Libiamo ne' lieti calici" ("Let's drink from the joyful cup") from Verdi's *La traviata*.

Track 53—Example from an oratorio: "Hallelujah Chorus" from Handel's *Messiah*.

Glossary

a cappella—An Italian term translated as "in chapel style," meaning vocalists sing without accompaniment. Today the term implies that a soloist, a small number of singers, or a chorus performs with no instrumental accompaniment.

accent marks—Staccato, staccatissimo, marcato, martelato, and tenuto. Dynamic accent marks give an extra emphasis to notes in varying degrees depending on which accent is used.

accidental—An intentional alteration of pitch within a piece of music. It is a half-step pitch change depending on the use of a natural, flat, or sharp. A natural cancels a flat or sharp. A flat lowers a note's pitch by a half step. A sharp raises a note's pitch by a half step. Accidentals produce chromatic alterations in music.

Acrobats of God—A 1960 orchestral score by Carlos Surinach that was commissioned by and dedicated to Martha Graham.

air—A free-form, lyrical, nondance movement often included in a baroque-era suite. The term originally meant a tune or a song.

allemande—A dance form originating in Germany during the Renaissance era (1400-1600 C.E.). Its music is a moderate duple or rapid triple meter. The name *allemande* is the French word for "German."

alto clef—See also *C clef*. The alto clef is used in music for the viola.

anglaise—A 17th-century French dance form from the late Middle Ages and early Renaissance era that evolved from English country dance. The name *Anglaise* is the French word for "English." Its music is in fast duple time, and the dance steps begin on the first beat. In the 18th century, the music form became a movement in some suites.

aria—A vocal solo usually from a musical work such as an opera or cantata from the Renaissance through the 21st century.

arpeggio—The notes of a chord played sequentially from the lowest notes of the chord (ascending) or from the highest note of the chord (descending).

articulation—The attack, release, and accent a note receives.

articulation markings—Indications of how to begin and end the playing or singing of a musical tone.

Asian tonality—Music based on a variety of tone systems depending upon the country's music era. Twelve-tone, five-tone (pentatonic), or seven-tone systems and scales are found in the music of China, Japan, Thailand, and Vietnam.

asymmetrical meter—Also referred to as uneven meter or composite meter. The beats within a measure can be grouped in twos, threes, or fours, such as in the time signature 5/4, in which the beats can be organized conventionally as 1-2, 3-4-5 or 1-2-3, 4-5. Less conventionally, the beats could be grouped as 1, 2-3, 4-5. Meters such as 7/8 and 11/8 are also examples of asymmetrical meters.

attack—A sound's beginning or how to play or sing a sound's beginning.

augmentation—A contrapuntal device that means a melody's notes are mathematically increased based on the original time value of a melody's notes. In augmentation (and diminution), a composer or arranger might change the time signature as well.

bar line—Initially, the vertical line at the beginning of a staff and that also follows the grand staff's brace. On a grand staff, the initial bar line looks like the subsequent bar lines and extends from the top treble staff line (F) to the bottom bass staff line (G).

bass clef—See also *F clef*. The bass clef designates staffs for lower-pitched brass instruments, the cello and double bass in the string family, baritone and bass men's voices, and keyboard music for the left hand.

beaming—The musical practice of connecting notes into groups designated by beams.

beams—Thick horizontal lines that connect repeated eighth, sixteenth, thirty-second notes, and so on. For groups of notes of the same value, beams serve the same time denotation as flags. For example, one beam is used for eighth notes, two beams for sixteenth notes, and so on.

beats—The number of pulses between regularly occurring accents. They divide time into specific durations.

binary form—A work that is divided into two distinct sections.

bourrée—A baroque-era court dance style that French King Louis XIV's court composer Jean Baptiste Lully created. It was usually written in duple time, with a rapid tempo, and in binary form. The melody usually begins on the third beat of a measure.

brace—The first symbol at the beginning of a grand staff composition. It resembles a left curly bracket and links the treble and bass staffs, indicating that the music notated on each staff should be played simultaneously.

bracket—The heavier vertical line that groups instruments together such as strings in an orchestral score.

bridge—A transitional section of a song, often between the A and B parts of the song.

cadence—The ending of a musical phrase. It is affected by melody, harmony, and rhythm and has two classifications: complete and incomplete.

canon—The strictest form of musical imitation. A canon starts when a melody begins; it may be vocal or instrumental. At a predetermined place in the first melody, a second voice or instrument begins and states the same melody exactly as the first voice.

canon inversion—An imitation technique in which a melodic inversion overlaps itself. In the context of canons, the term "inverted canon" is synonymous with "canon in contrary motion" (http://jan.ucc.nau.edu/tas3/canonanatomy.html).

cantata—A full-length vocal work for a chorus, soloists, and orchestra. The text of a cantata is biblical and is performed without scenery or costumes.

Cantique de Noël—In English, this traditional Christmas song is known as "O Holy Night." It was composed by the 19th-century ballet composer Adolphe Adam.

C clef—Also known as the alto clef. The C clef is a moveable clef that was used primarily in classical-era vocal and instrumental music, meaning music of the baroque, classical, and romantic periods. It is also used in the modern and contemporary periods for the instruments that require it. It is used in music for the viola, cello, bassoon, and trombone.

chaconne—A 16th-century Spanish dance form. In music the chaconne is a continuous variation form composed of musical variations written over a repeating bass line. It is based on a harmonic theme, a set of chords. Therefore, it has a multivoice harmonic ostinato. The repeating bass line form refers to the melodic, single-voiced ostinato and the harmonic ostinato of the chaconne.

chamber orchestra—Uses many of the instruments of the orchestra but in smaller numbers, often omitting some of the groups of a full orchestra.

character pieces—Short solo piano pieces from the 19th century which are often in binary form. Examples of character pieces include nocturnes, preludes, romances, intermezzi, fantasias, bagatelles, waltzes, mazurkas, and polonaises and were romantic-era compositions for virtuoso performance often presented in a private home, palace, chateau, or castle. Lesser character pieces (e.g., those that are overly sentimental) are also known as salon pieces.

chord—Three or more pitches played simultaneously and that produce various types of harmonies.

chorus—The section of a song that follows the verse. For each verse that is sung, a chorus usually follows. Also known as a refrain. Additionally the word *chorus* may refer to groups of singers.

clef—A symbol placed at the beginning of a staff that assigns specific pitches to the lines and spaces of the staff.

climax—A point at which the intensity of a phrase reaches a peak.

coda—An ending. In sonata allegro form, it is the first movement's ending section.

codetta—A shorter ending.

complete cadence—A conclusive end of a phrase. It gives the listener a sense that the phrase has ended.

composite meter—See *asymmetrical meter*.

compound meter—A time signature in which the beat unit divides into three equal parts. The bottom number will be the same as in simple meter, usually 2, 4, or 8 representing those note values which divide by two.

concerto—Usually a three-movement work for a solo instrument and an orchestra or chamber orchestra. It is a type of duet between the solo instrument and an orchestra.

conductor's score—See *full score*.

conjunct melodies—Melodies that move primarily by whole or half steps.

consonance—Sound created by intervals or chords that is harmonious or pleasant to the ear.

contrapuntal theme—A theme in which different versions of the theme occur simultaneously.

contrary motion—See also *inversion*. Going in the opposite direction. When a theme is inverted, the intervals go in the opposite direction.

contrast—Describes a melody, phrase, or theme that is different from a preceding melody, phrase, or theme.

counterpoint—Originated in the Middle Ages and describes the technique of writing polyphonic music or one voice of a multivoice texture in later periods (17th to 18th centuries).

courante—A court dance form originating in the Renaissance era in France. The music was slow, originally in 3/2 time, and then evolved to become fast paced.

da capo—Return to the beginning (in Italian, literally "to the head").

da capo aria—The operatic vocal form that evolved by the late 17th century and which contains two main sections: A and B. The B section is followed by the words "da capo" which direct the performers to the song's beginning, literally "to the head," to repeat the A section. The da capo aria is the vocal counterpart of the instrumental minuet and trio and was common in baroque-era opera.

development—The second component of sonata allegro form. In the development section of a movement, the composer applies various thematic treatments, manipulating and expanding the movement's theme(s).

diminution—A melodic counterpoint treatment in which a melody's note values are shortened. The composer or arranger determines the amount of the decrease in time.

disjunct melodies—Melodies with wider leaps between notes.

dissonance—Sound or harmonics created by intervals or chords that are inharmonious and jarring or that require resolution.

dot—Lengthens the value of a note or rest by half of the note's or rest's value.

dynamics—The intensity variances in the loudness or softness of music.

eighth note—Looks like a quarter note with a flag.

episode—A musical passage between statements of a main theme. Also another term for the digression from one section to the next.

exposition—The first component of sonata allegro form after the introduction. The composer uses the exposition to state the themes, the second of which includes a key change.

expression terms and symbols—Used in music to indicate the expressiveness that musicians should use when playing. They can indicate a general mood or tempo or a change of mood, tempo, volume, or quality.

fake book—A music book that contains melodies of jazz tunes or popular songs on a staff with the lyrics below and chords above the corresponding notes. Capital letters above the staff symbolize chords (e.g., A, G, F).

F clef—Also known as the bass clef and so named because it was derived from an old-fashioned letter F. On the bass staff, the two dots that follow the clef and which look like a colon appear above and below the F line, which is the fourth-highest line of the staff. The F clef designates staffs for lower-pitched brass instruments, cello, double bass, baritone and bass men's voices, and the left hand on keyboard music. It also moves to the D and A bass staff lines when used as the baritone and sub-bass clefs, respectively.

finite canon—A canon in which the composer has predetermined its length.

first-movement form—See *sonata allegro form.*

flags—Symbols that are placed at the top of stems that are on the right side of a note head or on the bottom of stems that descend from the left side of note heads. They indicate note values. For example, an eighth note has one flag, a sixteenth note has two flags, a thirty-second note has three flags, a sixty-fourth note has four flags, and so on, to a one-hundred twenty-eighth note.

flat— ♭ Symbol that lowers a pitch or tone by a half step and which looks similar to a lowercase letter b.

form—The outline, the overall design of a piece of music. It also refers to the overall organization of a piece of music.

fourth-movement form—May be theme and variations form, sonata allegro form, fantasy form (a free form), or rondo form.

free form—A form of music in which a composer determines the music's form. It means that the composer does not follow a standard form and structure.

French violin clef—Looks identical to the G, or treble, clef except that the clef moves to become centered on the E line, the lowest line of the treble staff.

fret—The small metal bar that divides a fret board into sections along the neck of the instrument and allows a musician to play different pitches by pressing specific fingers on specific strings between the frets.

full orchestra—Woodwinds (piccolos, flutes, clarinets, oboes, bassoons), brass (trumpets, trombones, French horns, tubas), strings (violins, violas, cellos, double basses), and percussion (drums, triangles, bells, and so on).

full score—Also known as the conductor's score. The original score in which every vocal or instrumental part appears individually.

gagaku—Classical Japanese court music dating to c. 800 C.E. It is still performed today and is called bugaku when it accompanies the Japanese classical court dance of the same name. Gagaku was not heard in the West until after World War II. For first-time listeners, it might be challenging to listen to because of its Asian tonality.

galanterien—Baroque-era court dances grouped in pairs.

gavotte—A French Renaissance-era court dance style that originated as a folk dance from the Dauphiné region in southeast France. Its duple-meter music endured through the 19th century as an instrumental form.

G clef—Also known as the treble clef. It is called the G clef because it resembles an old-fashioned letter G and crosses the staff's G line four times. It is used in music for higher-pitched voices and instruments such as violins, woodwinds, and the right hand on keyboard instruments. For the French violin, the G clef moves to become centered on the lowest line of the treble staff, E, and is called the French violin clef.

genre—A type (style) of music. May also be used to describe the various types or styles of dance.

gigue—An English dance form (jig) that was adopted by the French. Its music is in a rapid duple compound meter.

grand staff—Two staffs linked by a brace and bar line. It is the format of notation for keyboard music. Music for the piano, organ, harpsichord, clavichord, and electric and digital keyboards is notated on grand staffs.

Gregorian chant—In the history of Western music, the early Christian church adopted and adapted ancient Jewish and Islamic chants for the Mass. During the early medieval era, Pope Gregory I (c. 540-604 C.E.) called for these monophonic chants to be notated. This marked the beginning of Western music notation.

guitar tablature—Shows a musician how to play a chord with an illustration of which finger goes on which guitar fret.

half note—An open note head that is an oval-shaped, empty circle. The stem may ascend from the right side of the note head or descend from the left side of the note head.

half step—From one key to the very next on a piano keyboard (white note to white note, black note to white note, or white note to black note depending on the first note).

harmony—Occurs when two or more pitches sound at the same time. The sound created by the two or more pitches may be consonant (pleasant sounding or stable) or dissonant (incongruous, not well matched, or requiring resolution).

hertz—Taken from the name of the 19th-century physicist (Heinrich Hertz), who discovered the existence of sound wavelengths. Each pitch has a specified number of Hertz, abbreviated Hz, per second. The pitch of A above middle C, for example, vibrates at 440 Hz.

homophony—A musical texture based on a melody and its accompanying harmonies.

imitation—Each voice (vocal or instrumental) uses the same melodic material as it enters the musical fabric.

imitative counterpoint—Includes canons and rounds, where instruments or voices repeat the melody in specific, overlapping time intervals.

incomplete cadence—A phrase ending that indicates the music will continue.

inconclusive cadence—See *incomplete cadence*.

infinite canon—Commonly known as a round and is usually repeated many times.

interval—The distance from a lower tone to higher tone or from a higher tone to a lower tone; the distance between two pitches. Musicians count the first and last tone in an interval.

inversion—In counterpoint, turning the melodic contour in the opposite direction from its original statement. Inversion may also be applied to a single interval.

key—The tonality of a piece of music determined by the first pitch of the scale upon which it is based.

keyboard music—Music for the piano, organ, harpsichord, clavichord, and electric and digital keyboards that is notated on a grand staff.

key signatures—Specific groupings of sharps or flats on the staff head or the beginning of each staff in a composition with the exception of the key of C, which has no sharps or flats. A key signature, therefore, might have no sharps or flats or up to seven sharps or flats.

ledger lines—Indicate pitches that are lower or higher than those represented on the five lines and four spaces of the staff. They are short lines that appear to extend to the right and left of the note when in actuality the note is placed on the short line above or below the staff.

legato—Literally means "bound" in Italian. It is the norm for musicians and refers to smooth movement from one note to the next.

loure—A French baroque-era court dance form whose music is written in triple meter. Well-known composers of loures are Jean Baptiste Lully and J.S. Bach.

madrigal—An unaccompanied, contrapuntal secular song dating to the late Middle Ages.

major—Literally means "greater" in Latin. It refers to one of the two modes of Western music and the tonality or relationship of pitch patterns of the tones of the major scales. Music written in the major mode sounds happy or cheerful. The major scales are represented in the major keys for which they are named and also represent the harmonic relationship of the seven pitches of the major scales. The key of C is a major key. The naming of the key of C centers on the fact that the C scale begins and ends on the pitch of C. The seven pitches of the key of C are based on the harmonic relationship of the C-scale pitches.

major scale—The specified series of pitches of any of the major keys. Any scale following the step pattern of two whole steps, a half step, three whole steps, and a half step is a major scale. The first pitch of the scale names the scale.

marcato— $>$ Literally means "marked." As a dynamic accent symbol, marcato looks like a mathematical greater-than symbol. Marcato symbols are placed above or below the note head to indicate that the playing of the note is louder and more stressed than usual.

march—A music style often played in concerts, marched to by marching bands, and heard and seen in parades as well as at halftime during football games.

martelato— $\wedge$ A dynamic accent mark that literally means "hammered" and is indicated by an inverted-V symbol. Martelato indicates that a note should be played forcefully (see table 1.4).

mass—Music form based on the sequence of the religious service. Its five components are the kyrie, gloria, credo, sanctus, and agnus dei.

melodic sequence—When a motive is repeated beginning on different (usually successive) pitches. The repetition on different, successive pitches creates a melodic sequence.

melodic structure—Melody made up of motives, phrases, a climax, and a cadence.

meter—A series of pulses receiving a regularly occurring accent on count 1, which then designates them as beats.

meter signature—See *time signature*.

metrical accent—Placing an accent on the first beat of a group of beats.

metronome—A device or application that provides a regular beat and may also designate the first beat of a measure.

middle C—Denotes the center of the grand staff and is the most central C on the piano keyboard. It is the fourth C pitch on the piano keyboard (counting from the left end of the keyboard).

minor—Literally means "lesser" or "smaller" in Latin. Minor refers to one of the two modes in Western music and the tonality or relationship of pitch patterns of minor scale tones. Minor mode music sounds melancholy or brooding. There are three minor modes in Western music: natural, harmonic, and melodic. Each minor mode has a specified pattern of whole and half steps, based on the natural, harmonic, or melodic minor scales.

minor scale—All minor scales have a lowered third pitch. The minor keys refer to any scale following a minor mode step pattern. There are three minor scales, the natural, the melodic, and the harmonic. The natural minor scale has half steps between the second and third notes and the fifth and sixth notes. The harmonic minor raises the seventh note. The melodic minor raises the sixth and seventh note when ascending and lowers them (returning to natural minor) when descending.

minuet—A court dance form from the late baroque era whose originator is disputed (some say Jean Baptiste Lully created the form while others say Louis Pécour was its creator). It was a moderate-tempo triple-meter dance that evolved into the waltz in the 19th century. Many composers used the musical form for the third movement of symphonies.

minuet and trio—A ternary music form (ABA) that evolved from how minuets were grouped in pairs during the baroque era. A first minuet was played with some or all of its sections being repeated. Then a second minuet was played, originally by only three musicians. When the second minuet finished, the first minuet was played again without any of its sections being repeated. Composers in the 18th century adopted the minuet and trio ternary form for the third movement in their symphonies.

mixed meters—Measures or groupings of measures in different time signatures.

modulation—Moving from one key to another within a song or a piece of music.

monophony—Classifies music composed of only a single melodic line. A melody heard alone with no other voices or melodic instruments is monophonic. Monophony may also be voices singing in unison or instruments playing in unison.

motet—From the late Middle Ages, a contrapuntal vocal form for two or more voices that was based on biblical text.

motive—One element of melodic structure. If present as a melodic component, it is a short group of notes arranged in a distinctive melodic, rhythmic, or melodic–rhythmic pattern or design.

movement—A melody's pace, how quickly it combines or divides beats. Also describes a main section of a longer musical work such as a symphony, concerto, mass, oratorio, cantata, suite, string quartet, or sonata. Movements are considered closed in form, meaning that they can stand alone harmonically and as a form. They can also be divided into sections themselves.

musical time—The organization of music through pulse, meter, and rhythm.

music score—Staffs with every voice's or instrument's part listed with all of the composer's directions on how the parts should be performed (e.g., using notations such as tempo terms and symbols, dynamic markings, and expression markings). A score may be for one instrument or for every conceivable number and combination of instruments and voices.

natural— ♮ A symbol that is placed in front of a particular note and cancels any previous sharp or flat for that pitch in a particular measure. It may also cancel a key-signature sharp or flat in any measure of a composition.

neoclassicism—Refers to the influence of classicism's precepts on composers in the early to mid-20th century. In music, classicism's precepts were beauty, order, clarity, restrained emotion, and succinct statement (the classical era in music was approximately 1750 to 1820 C.E.). Neoclassic music blends classicism with contemporary music ideas.

nonimitative counterpoint—Simultaneously occurring melodies. The melodies do not have to coincide or match in rhythm, time, or key. They merely occur simultaneously.

nonimitative polyphony—When different melodies occur at the same time within the same key or related keys. Musicians may be playing in the same key and meter, yet their melodies may or may not be related. If the melodies are not related, then what they are doing is called nonimitative polyphony.

notation—A combination of terms, symbols (including notes), and signs that enables musicians to reproduce music as the composer wrote it and in the way that he or she wished for it to be heard.

note—A symbol used to designate the pitch and time value of a tone. The time value is based on the time signature.

octave—Means "eight." From one C to the next is eight tones; an interval of eight tones is an octave.

octet—A song or piece of music for eight voices or instruments.

open-ended melody—An incomplete melody; it leads the listener to expect more. Open-ended melodies are often the building blocks for longer songs or themes.

opera—A dramatic or comic stage production with costuming and sets. It is a production for a chorus and solo vocalists who sing and act out an elaborate story set to orchestral accompaniment.

oratorio—A full-length vocal work for a chorus, soloists, and orchestra. The text of an oratorio is biblical and is usually performed without scenery or costumes.

ostinato—Repeated bass, melodic, or harmonic patterns.

ostinato forms—Music forms based on the late Renaissance dance forms of the chaconne and the passacaglia.

passacaglia—A 17th-century Spanish dance form. It is a continuous variation form of musical variations written over a repeating bass line. The passacaglia has a melodic, single-voiced ostinato with no harmonies in its first entry.

passepied—A French baroque dance form whose music is written in a quick triple meter.

pentatonic scale—A musical scale of five tones in which the octave is reached at the sixth tone; a scale in which the tones are arranged like a major scale with its fourth and seventh tones omitted.

perpetual canon—See *infinite canon*.

phrase—An element of a melody; similar to a sentence in language. Phrases vary in length depending on the musical composition.

phrasing—Notes of a melody linked as a musical thought and played or sung as a grouping.

piano score—A series of grand staffs; music for the piano.

pitch—Refers to the highness or lowness of tones determined by their frequency.

polonaise—A Polish court processional dance form originating in the 17th century. It is in a moderate triple meter with a strong accent on the first beat of each measure.

polymeter—The simultaneous occurrence of two or more meters.

polyphonic simultaneity—Occurs when dissimilar melodies sound at the same time. They do not have to be in the same key, share the same time signature, or have any other musical elements in common.

polyphony—Consists of at least two independent melodies that are approximately equal in importance within a piece of music. The melodies' resultant harmonies and rhythms add interest to the polyphony. Polyphony has two or more melodies sounding at the same time. Applies to early music (15th and 16th centuries).

prelude—An introductory musical section or a short musical piece that may stand alone.

pulse—A regularly occurring beat with no organizing accents.

quarter note—A black note head (filled-in oval circle) with a stem ascending from the right side or descending from the left side.

quartet—Four instruments or voices or the music for four instruments or voices. The instrumentation for a string quartet is usually two violins, a viola, and a cello.

quintet—Five instruments or voices or the music for five instruments or voices. A classical-era quintet typically calls for two violins, two violas, and a cello, or two violins, one viola, and two cellos.

quodlibet—The simultaneous performance of well-known tunes which often complement each other harmonically and rhythmically.

range—Describes a melody's highest and lowest pitches. Generally refers to how together (narrow) or apart (wide) a melody's notes are. Range may also refer to a singer's range or the range of an instrument describing their highest and lowest pitches.

recapitulation—The third section of sonata allegro form. In the recapitulation, the composer restates the original theme(s). The recapitulation may be literal or varied.

recitative—A style of singing in which the singer uses the rhythms of ordinary speech so that exposition may be delivered or the plot of an opera moved forward quickly.

refrain—See *chorus.*

rehearsal letters—May appear above the staffs of a longer music work. Rehearsal letters or actual bar numbers may appear intermittently throughout a work. These letters or numbers give the conductor and musicians reference points at which they can resume playing together in rehearsal. In a long work, rehearsal letters may signify distinct sections of the composition. Also known as rehearsal marks or rehearsal figures.

release—The ending of a tone.

répétiteur—The French term for the person who rehearses (or stages) a dance work.

repetition—The restatement of a melody, phrase, or theme in music. Repetition may be literal, meaning exactly the same, or it may be varied. Repetition can be used to create longer, more developed works.

restatement—The first part of a song or musical work (A) is repeated after a contrasting section (B).

retrograde—A form of melodic manipulation in which the melody's pitches occur in a backward sequence beginning with the last note and moving backward through the melody to the first note.

retrograde inversion—A musical structure and melodic manipulation technique that is performed from last note to first with the intervals inverted beginning with the last note and moving backward through the composition or phrase to the first note.

rhythm—A combination of short and long sounds created by combining or dividing beats. It may be melodic (created on an instrument or by a voice) or percussive (as played on drums or other percussion instruments).

rigaudon—A baroque-era French court dance that originated in the southeast of France. Its music is in a fast duple meter.

ritornello—A short, recurring passage.

ritornello form—Baroque musical form that includes a short, recurring passage.

rondo—Form that is composed of at least three sections (A, B, and C). The A, B, and C sections are performed in the order of ABACA. *Rondo* means return and it is the return of the A theme that gives this form its name.

round—See *infinite canon.*

sarabande—A Spanish baroque-era court dance. Its music is in a slow triple meter with an accent on the second beat.

scale—A series of eight alphabetically named pitches, which usually progress by specified steps and half steps. The name of the scale is determined by the name of its beginning pitch. For example, a C scale begins on the pitch of C.

scherzo—Literally means "joke" in Italian. In some 19th-century symphonies, the minuet of the third movement was replaced by a scherzo movement, a quick-paced movement in 3/4 time.

second-movement form—Changes key and tempo from the first movement, has an emphasis on lyric melody, and is often in a theme and variations form. A second movement may also be free form, sonata form, rondo form, or ternary form.

self-contained melody—A melody in songs or short instrumental pieces that is complete unto itself.

sharp—♯ A symbol that looks similar to the pound or number sign and indicates a pitch should be raised by a half step.

simple meter—A time signature in which the top number is always two, three, or four and the beat unit can be divided into two equal parts.

sixteenth note—Looks like a quarter note with two flags.

slur—An articulation term and symbol that reminds musicians or singers to play or sing in a legato manner. Specifically it is a slightly curved line above or below two or more notes. In vocal music, a slur indicates that the slurred notes should be sung with one breath.

sonata—Originally a composition that was to be played as opposed to a cantata, a composition that was to be sung. Since the classical period, it is a multimovement work with at least one movement in sonata allegro form. It is now a composition or piece of music for a solo instrument or a solo instrument with piano accompaniment.

sonata allegro form—There are four components to sonata allegro form, which is also known as first-movement form: exposition, development, recapitulation, and coda.

sonata form—See *sonata allegro form.*

staccatissimo—▾ Means "most staccato." Staccatissimo symbols look similar to a straight apostrophe. They are placed above or below but not touching the note head. Staccatissimo notes are played or sung as extremely detached or separated from each other.

staccato—• Means "detached." The symbol for staccato is a dot above or below the note head. Staccato notes are played or sung with a sense of detachment from each other.

staff—A horizontal grouping of five lines and resultant four spaces between the five lines.

stem—A short, straight line attached to the right or left side of a note head.

stress—An extra emphasis occurring on any beat.

string quartet score—Has four staffs, one for each instrument of the string quartet: two violins, a viola, and a cello.

structure—Refers not only to the tonal or harmonic organization of a piece of music but also to the components of the form. Structure involves the details of the overall design of a piece of music. A work's structure reveals the way in which a composer created and linked sections.

subdivide—To divide notes or beats according to the music's time signature.

suite—A musical work grouping movements that originated as dance styles.

symphony—A multimovement musical composition for orchestra in which at least one movement is in sonata allegro form.

symphony orchestra—May have up to 100 musicians playing the instruments from the woodwind, brass, percussion, and string families.

tempo—An Italian term that describes the rate of speed of the music or dance. It indicates how quickly the beats of the music progress.

tenuto— ▬ Means "to hold." It is a dynamic accent symbol that looks like a dash above or below a note head. Unlike the other dynamic accent marks, tenuto is a pressure accent. When applied to the playing or singing of a note, the musician or singer gives the note a slight stress and holds the note to its full value.

ternary form—A song, a movement of a multimovement work, or an operatic aria that has three distinct and complete sections.

texture—Describes how a composer combines a composition's elements or components. Texture also describes the music's depth and richness of sound.

theme—A melody in a musical composition.

theme and variations—Also known as *variations on a theme*. A form that expands a musical idea to create a longer work through either sectional (pauses after each variation) or continuous variations where one variation leads into the next.

third-movement form—A form based on the minuet and trio. In the 19th century, Beethoven added an option of using a scherzo and trio for third-movement form.

tie—A curved line connecting two notes of the same pitch, but it does not touch the two notes. It indicates that a pitch should be held for the combined value of the two notes. A tie may link notes within the same measure so that the notes' values are combined within the measure. It may also extend the duration of a note into the following measure.

time signature—Tells musicians how many beats are in a measure and what type of note receives one beat.

tonality—Refers to the key center of a piece of music. In Western music it refers to the use of major and minor keys, which are based on the major and minor scales.

tonic pitch—The first pitch of any major or minor scale. The tonic pitch names the scale and gives the key its name. For example, the key of A is so named because the tonic pitch, the first pitch of the scale, is A.

treble clef—See *G clef*.

trio—Music for three voices or instruments; also the second section of a scherzo or minuet movement.

triplet—Three notes played in the time of two notes of the same value or in the time value of one note of the next larger value.

two-step—An early 20th-century popular dance form (also known as the cakewalk) whose title has evolved to describe a current country-western dance form (Texas two-step) in which partners two-step counterclockwise with a variant of ballroom dance's closed position while moving in a circular formation around a dance floor.

uneven meter—See *asymmetrical meter* and *composite meter*.

variation form—See *theme and variations*.

verse—The first part of a song; after the chorus the verse is repeated with different lyrics as many times there are different lyrics. Hymns and Christmas carols exemplify this kind of structure.

whole note—A note that looks like a small, empty, slightly oval circle known as an open note head.

whole step—A skipping of one key on a piano keyboard.

whole-tone scale—A musical scale progressing by whole steps.

References and Resources

Adam, A. (1935). Cantique de Noël [O holy night]. New York: Schirmer. (Originally published 1847.)

Adam, A. (1847). *O holy night*. New York: Schirmer.

Adams, W., Gomez, J., Pajon, G., & Curtis, J. (2003). Shut Up remix. *The E.N.D. (Energy Never Dies)* [CD, deluxe edition]. Santa Monica: Interscope Records, Universal Music Group.

Alvira, J.R. (2011). Quarendo invenietis canon from Bach's *Musical offering* (*Musicalisches opfer*), BWV 1079. www.teoria.com/reference/l/inversion_counter.php.

Apple, Fiona. (2005). Extraordinary machine. *Extraordinary machine* [CD and DVD]. New York: Sony BMG Music.

ArtsAlive.ca. (2010). http:/artsalive.ca/en/dan/make/toolbox/solo.asp.

Bach, J.S. (c. 1948). Prelude in C, no. 1. *The well-tempered clavier*, BWV 846. *Piano pieces the whole world plays* (vol. 2). New York: Appleton-Century-Crofts. (Originally published 1722.)

Bach, J.S. (1927). Two part invention no. 1, BWV 772. New York: Schirmer. (Originally published 1722.)

Bach, J.S., & Gounod, C. (1859). Ave Maria.

Baker, T. (1947). *Pronouncing pocket-manual of musical terms*. New York: Schirmer.

Beethoven, L.V. (1949). Symphony no. 5 in C minor, op. 67 [Cond. Carl Schuricht, Paris Conservatory Orchestra]. *Beethoven Symphony no. 5 in C minor, op. 67* [Vinyl LP]. New York: London Gramophone. (Originally published in 1808.)

Benward, B. (1985). *Music in theory and practice*. Dubuque, IA: Brown.

Berlin, I. (1919). A pretty girl is like a melody. www.stlyrics.com/lyrics/blueskies/aprettygirlislikeamelody. htm and http://enwikisource.org/wiki/A_pretty_girl_is_like_a_melody.

Bernstein, L. (2002). America. *West side story*. New York: Leonard Bernstein Music. (Originally published 1957.)

Berry, W. (1986). *Form in music*. New York: Alfred.

Bierley, P.E. (2007). John Philip Sousa [biography] Performing arts encyclopedia, Library of Congress. http://lcweb2.loc.gov/diglib/ihas/loc.natlib.ihas.200152755/default.html.

Blood, B. (2011). Music theory online: Phrasing and articulation, lesson 21. www.Dolmetsch.com/musictheory21.htm#staccato.

Brandt, A. (2007, September 24). *Musical identity*. http://cnx.org/content/m15158/1.1.

Bullivant, R. (1995). Augmentation. In S. Sadie (Ed.), *The New Grove dictionary of music and musicians*. London: MacMillan.

Cars. (1981). Touch and go. *Down boys* [Vinyl LP]. New York: Elektra 47039.

Chopin, F. (1945). Polonaise, op. 26, no. 1 in C-sharp minor. In Samuel Spivak (Ed.). *Everybody's favorite Chopin album*. No. 56. New York: Amsco Music. (Originally published 1836.)

Chopin, F. (1972). Variations in B flat, op. 2. [Cond. Eliahu Inbal, London Philharmonic Orchestra]. *Chopin: Andante spianato and other works* [Cassette Tape]. New York: Philips 7300 198. (Originally published 1827.)

Chopin, F. (1824). Variationen über ein thema von Rossini in E major, KK Anh.Ia/5 (B. 9) [Cond. Charles Gerhardt, National Philharmonic Orchestra]. *Magic flute* [CD]. New York: RCA. (1992).

Cooper, G.W., & Meyer, L.B. (1960). *The rhythmic structure of music*. Chicago: University of Chicago Press.

Cranberries. (1994). Zombie. *No need to argue*. London: PolyGram Records.

Croft, I., & Fraser, D. (1985). *A dictionary of musical quotations*. New York: Schirmer Books, MacMillan, Inc.

Crow, S. (1993). All I wanna do. *Tuesday night music club* [CD]. Hollywood: A&M Records.

Crumb, George. (N.d.). Music: Does it have a future? www.georgecrumb.net/future.html.

DaCosta, Morton (Director). (1962). Pick a little talk a little. *The music man* [Motion Picture]. Los Angeles: Warner Brothers.

Dance Heritage Coalition. (2010). Fred Astaire. www.danceheritage.org/astaire.html.

Demuth, N. (1953). *Musical forms and textures*. London: Rockliff.

Dolmetsch. (2011). Musical symbols.\dblspace\www.Dolmetsch.com/musical symbols.htm.

Drabkin, W. (1995). Inversion. In S. Sadie (Ed.), *The New Grove dictionary of music and musicians*. London: MacMillan.

Dürr, W., & Gerstenberg, W. (1980). Rhythm. In S. Sadie (Ed.), *The New Grove dictionary of music and musicians* (6th ed., vol. 15). London: Macmillan.

Edwards, A.C. (1956). *The art of melody*. New York: Philosophical Library.

Ellington, D. (1993). C-jam blues. *Homage to Duke* [CD]. New York: GRP Records. GRD 9715, Verve Music Group. (Originally published 1941.)

Ellington, D., & Bigard, B. (1993). Mood indigo. *Homage to Duke* [CD]. New York: GRP Records. GRD 9715, Verve Music Group. (Originally published 1930.)

Erickson, R. (1955). *The structure of music: A listener's guide*. New York: Noonday Press.

Falla, Manuel de. (n.d.). Ritual fire dance from *El amor brujo* (*Love the magician*). [Cond. Eugene Ormandy, Philadelphia Orchestra]. *Ormandy, Philadelphia Orchestra's Greatest Hits* [Vinyl LP]. New York: Columbia MS 6934. (Originally published 1915.)

Fauré, G. (1887). Pavane for Orchestra and Chorus ad lib in F sharp minor [Cond. Claus Ogerman, Columbia Symphony Orchestra]. *Classical Barbra* [CD]. New York: Sony. (1990).

Fiske, R. (1959). *Orchestration. Score reading*, vol 1. New York: Oxford University Press.

Forney, K. & Machlis, J. (2011). *The enjoyment of music* (11th ed.). New York: Norton.

Fox-Strangways, A.H. (1954). Time. In E. Blom (Ed.), *Grove's dictionary of music and musicians* (5th ed.), vol. 8. 20 vols. New York: Macmillan.

Frobenius, W. (1995). Texture. In S. Sadie (Ed.), *The New Grove dictionary of music and musicians*, vol. 15. London: MacMillan.

Glass, P. (2006). *Symphony No. 8*. www.philipglass.com/music/recordings/symphony_8.php.

Green, D.M. (1965). *Form in tonal music*. New York: Holt.

Harrell, T., Knowles, B., Stewart, C., & Nash, T. (2009). Single ladies. *I Am . . . Sasha Fierce* [CD]. New York: Sony.

Harrison, G. (1969). Something. *Abbey Road* [Vinyl LP]. London: Apple Records SO-383.

Hendrix, J. (1967). Purple haze. *Are you experienced?* [Vinyl LP]. Santa Monica: MCA Records.

Hopkins, A. (1982). *Sounds of music*. London: Dent.

Humphrey, D. (1959). *The art of making dances*. New York: Grove Press.

Jacob, G. (1944). *How to read a score*. London: Hawkes.

Jobim, A.C., & Lees, G. (1964). Corcovado (Quiet Nights of Quiet Stars). *Getz au Go Go* [CD]. New York: Verve Records 821725-2. (Originally published 1960.)

Jobim, A.C., Lees, G., Mendonça, Newton, & Hendricks, Jon. (1963). One note samba. *Getz au go go* [CD]. New York: Verve Records 821725-2. (1964)

Kerman, J., with Kerman, V. (1992). *Listen*. 2nd Brief ed. New York: Worth.

Lennon, J., & McCartney, P. (1968). Hey Jude. *Abbey road* [Vinyl LP]. London: Apple Records, SO-383.

Lester, J. (1986). *The rhythms of tonal music*. Carbondale: Southern Illinois University Press.

Liné, H.S. (1902). *Belle of Richmond*. New York: Stern.

Linsley, D.E. (2008). *Melodic inversion in J.S. Bach's keyboard suites*. Master's thesis. University of Oregon. https://scholarsbank.uoregon.edu/xmlui/bitstream/handle/1794/7770/Linsley_Dennis_Edward_MA_spring2008.pdf?sequence=1.

Louvrien, D. (2011). A brief timeline of Sousa's life. Dallas Wind Symphony. www.dws.org/sousa/learn/timeline.

MacDonald, H. (2001). Scherzo. In S. Sadie (Ed.), *The New Grove dictionary of music and musicians,* vol. 22. London: Macmillan.

Machlis, J., with Forney, K. (1991). *The enjoyment of music* (6th ed.). New York: Norton.

Manoff, T. (1982). *Music: A living language.* New York: Norton.

Marks, M. (1971, March). Like trying to explain color to a blind person: Trude Rittmann talks about the musical illiteracy of dancers. *Dance Magazine.*

Melcher, R.A., & Warch, W.F. (1971). *Music for score reading.* Englewood Cliffs, NJ: Prentice-Hall.

Monroe, M. (2008). Bach's crab canon. http://wn.com/MMmusing.

Mozart, W.A. (1970). Quartet no. 13 in D minor, K. 173. *Wolfgang Amadeus Mozart complete string quartets.* New York: Dover. (Originally published 1773.)

Mozart, Wolfgang A. (c. 1948). Turkish march. *Piano pieces the whole world plays* (vol. 2). New York: Appleton-Century-Crofts. (Originally published c. 1783.)

Mozart, W.A. (1900). Violin concerto no. 1 in B flat major, K. 207. New York: Kalmus. (Originally published 1775.)

Moulton, B. (15 July 1993). Lecture on form. Norman, OK: Regional Dance America's 1993 National Choreographers' Conference, University of Oklahoma.

Nunlist, Juli. (1964, August). Music: Your silent partner. *Dance Magazine.*

Osborne, J. (1995). Right hand man. *Relish* [CD]. New York: UMG.

Owen, H. (1992). *Modal and tonal counterpoint.* New York: Schirmer.

Politoske, David T. (1974). *Music.* Englewood Cliffs, NJ: Prentice-Hall.

Porter, C. (1973). Night and day. *Gay divorce.* New York: Quadrangle. (Originally published 1932 by Harms.)

Rachmaninoff, S. (c. 1948). Prelude in C sharp minor op. 3, no. 2. *Piano pieces the whole world plays,* vol. 2. New York: Appleton-Century-Crofts. (Originally published 1893.)

Rachmaninoff, Serge. (1912). Vocalise, op. 34, no. 14.

Randel, D.M. (Ed.). (1986). *The New Harvard dictionary of music.* Cambridge, MA: Harvard University Press, Belknap Press.

Rodgers, R., & Hammerstein, O. (1965). Do-re-mi [Cond. Irwin Kostal]. *The sound of music* [Vinyl LP]. New York: RCA Victor, LSOD-2005. (Originally published 1959.)

Ryman, R. (1999). Benesh movement notation of the lilac fairy variation prologue, *The Sleeping Beauty.*

Sadie, S. (Ed.). (1995). *The New Grove dictionary of music and musicians,* 20 vols. London: MacMillan.

Scharwenka, X. (c. 1948). Polish dance in E flat minor, op. 3, no. 1. *Piano pieces the whole world plays,* vol. 2. New York: Appleton. (Originally published c. 1877.)

Siegmeister, E. (1965). *Harmony and melody,* vol. 1. Belmont: Wadsworth.

Sinatra, Frank (1991). The best is yet to come. *Sinatra reprise: The very good years.* New York: Warner Bros. (Originally recorded 1964.)

SPARK Educator Guide. Alonzo King (N.d.). www.kqed.org/assets/pdf/arts/programs/spark/211.pdf?trackurl=true.

Sting. (1993). Love is stronger than justice. *Ten summoner's tales.* Hollywood: A&M Records.

Surinach, C. (1972). *Acrobats of God.* New York: Associated Music.

Takasago, K. (N.d.). Kyoto Imperial Court Music Orchestra. www.discogs.com/Kyoto-Imperial-Court-Music-Of-Japan/release/2425753.

Tchaikovsky, P.I. (1950). *La belle au bois dormant* [*The sleeping beauty*] op. 66, piano score (Alexander Siloti, Arr.; Peter March, Ed.). New York: Tchaikovsky Foundation. (Originally published c. 1890.)

Tchaikovsky, P.I. (N.d.). *Violin Concerto* in D major, op. 35. New York: Edwin F. Kalmus [No. L331]. (Originally published 1878.)

Tilmouth, M. (1995). Binary form. In S. Sadie (Ed.), *The New Grove dictionary of music and musicians,* vol. 2. London: Macmillan.

Turek, R. (1988). *The elements of music: Concepts and applications* (vol. 1). New York: McGraw-Hill.

Tyndall, Robert E. (1964). *Musical form.* Boston: Allyn and Bacon.

Wagner, Richard. (1914). Bridal procession from Lohengrin. *The most popular piano pieces,* vol II. New York: Hinds. (Originally published c. 1850.)

Walton, C.W. (1974). *Basic forms in music.* New York: Alfred.

Weissman, Dick. (1994). *Creating melodies.* Cincinnati: Writer's Digest Books.

Welsh, G. (2000). Didn't leave nobody but the baby. *O brother, where art thou* [CD]. Nashville: Lost Highway Records.

Westrup, J.A., & Harrison, F.U. (1976). *The New College encyclopedia of music.* Revised by Conrad Wilson. New York: Norton.

White, J.D. (1995). Theories of musical texture in western history. Vol. 1 of *Perspectives in music criticism and theory,* vol. 1678 of *Garland reference library of the humanities.* New York: Garland.

Whittall, A. (1995). Form. In S. Sadie (Ed.), *The New Grove Dictionary of Music and Musicians,* vol. 6. London: Macmillan.

Wolf, E.K. (1986). Binary and ternary form. In D.M. Randel (Ed.), *The New Harvard Dictionary of Music.* Cambridge, MA: Harvard University Press, Belknap Press.

Zappa, F. (1970). Toads of the short forest. The Mothers of Invention's *Weasels ripped my flesh* [Vinyl LP]. New York: Warner Bros. Reprise Records MS 2028.

Index

Note: Page references followed by an italicized *f* indicate information contained in figures.

About the Author

Nola Nolen Holland, MFA, is an assistant professor in the department of dance at Slippery Rock University of Pennsylvania. For 10 years Nolen Holland taught courses in music for dance. Her search for a music text written specifically for dancers led her to create *Music Fundamentals for Dance.*

An experienced dancer, dance educator, and choreographer, Nolen Holland danced in Pittsburgh Ballet Theatre and has collaborated with composers to create original music for her dance compositions. She is the 2012-2014 president of CORPS de Ballet International, Inc., a professional organization for ballet teachers in higher education.

Recognition for Nolen Holland's choreography includes presentation of her work at the 1992 American College Dance Festival National Gala, the 1994 5th Biennial International University Dance Festival at the Université Lumière in Lyon, France, and the 2007 International Dance Alliance in Chennai, India.

You'll find other outstanding
dance resources at
www.HumanKinetics.com

In the U.S. call 1.800.747.4457
Australia 08 8372 0999
Canada. 1.800.465.7301
Europe . . . . .+44 (0) 113 255 5665
New Zealand 0800 222 062

HUMAN KINETICS
The Information Leader in Physical Activity & Health
P.O. Box 5076 • Champaign, IL 61825-5076